I0448656

July 2013

GLOBAL MANUFACTURING

Foreign Government Programs Differ in Some Key Respects From Those in the United States

GAO-13-365

July 2013

GLOBAL MANUFACTURING

Foreign Government Programs Differ in Some Key Respects from Those in the United States

Highlights of GAO-13-365, a report to the Chairman, Committee on Commerce, Science, and Transportation, U.S. Senate

Why GAO Did This Study

Over the last decade, the United States lost about one-third of its manufacturing jobs, raising concerns about U.S. manufacturing competitiveness. There may be insights to glean from government policies of similarly-situated countries, which are facing some of the same challenges of increased competition in manufacturing from developing countries.

GAO was asked to identify innovative foreign programs that support manufacturing that may help inform U.S. policy. Specifically, GAO examined (1) government strategies and programs other advanced economies have implemented to approach issues similar to those facing U.S. manufacturing, and (2) the key distinctions between government approaches to support manufacturing in other advanced economies and those in the United States. Based on input from experts and federal officials, and an analysis of manufacturing programs in other advanced countries, GAO selected Canada, Germany, Japan, and South Korea for study. In each country, GAO interviewed program officials and reviewed documents describing their programs. To identify distinctions between foreign and U.S. approaches to supporting manufacturing, GAO researched comparable programs in the United States, and interviewed staff administering those programs.

GAO is not making any recommendations in this report. GAO received only technical comments on this report from federal agencies.

View GAO-13-365. For more information, contact Andrew Sherrill at (202) 512-7215 or SherrillA@gao.gov or Lawrance Evans at (202) 512-4802 or EvansL@gao.gov.

What GAO Found

The four countries GAO analyzed—Canada, Germany, Japan, and South Korea—offer a varied mix of programs to support their manufacturing sectors. For example, Canada is shifting emphasis from its primary research and development (R&D) tax credit toward direct support to manufacturers to encourage innovation, particularly small- and medium-sized enterprises (SMEs). Germany has established applied institutes and clusters of researchers and manufacturers to conduct R&D in priority areas, as well as a national dual training system that combines classroom study with workplace training, and develops national vocational skills standards and credentials in 350 occupations. Japan has implemented science and technology programs—with a major focus on alternative energy projects—as part of a comprehensive manufacturing strategy. South Korea has substantially expanded investments in R&D, including the development of a network of technoparks—regional innovation centers that provide R&D facilities, business incubation, and education and production assistance to industry.

When compared to the United States, the countries in GAO's study offer some key distinctions in government programs to support the manufacturing sector in the areas of innovation, trade, and training.

- While the United States and the other four countries all provide support for innovation and R&D, the foreign programs place greater emphasis on commercialization to help manufacturers bridge the gap between innovative ideas and sales. These include programs that support infrastructure as well as hands-on technical and product development services to firms, and that foster collaboration between manufacturers and researchers. In contrast, the United States relies heavily on competitive funding for R&D projects with commercial potential.
- Within trade policy, the United States and the four countries in GAO's study provide similar services, but there are several differences in how they are delivered. For example, the United States is an acknowledged leader in intellectual property protection, but the U.S. government plays a less prominent role than the Japanese government in developing technological standards on industrial products.
- A key difference related to training programs pertains to the sustained role of government in coordinating stakeholder input into a national system of vocational skills training and credentialing, which helps provide a supply of skilled workers for manufacturers. This was particularly evident in Germany. In contrast, the United States largely devolves vocational training to states and localities and does not have a national system to issue industry-recognized credentials. However, the U.S. manufacturing industry, with participation from the federal government, has recently launched an effort to establish nationally portable, industry-recognized credentials for the manufacturing sector.

Overall, GAO's analysis shows the broad extent to which four countries who are U.S. competitors are leveraging the public sector to help their manufacturing industries maintain competitiveness in a rapidly changing global economy.

_____ **United States Government Accountability Office**

Contents

Letter		1
	Background	3
	Other Economically Advanced Countries Have Instituted a Varied Mix of Programs to Address Key Manufacturing Issues in Their Countries	11
	Foreign Manufacturing Programs Offer Some Key Contrasts to Those in the United States	26
	Concluding Observations	40
	Agency and Third-Party Comments and Our Evaluation	41
Appendix I	Objectives, Scope, and Methodology	43
Appendix II	Examples of Recent U.S. Manufacturing Policy Initiatives	46
Appendix III	Examples of Government Programs that Support Manufacturing in Canada, Germany, Japan, and South Korea	49
Appendix IV	GAO Contacts and Staff Acknowledgments	71
Related GAO Products		72

Tables

Table 1: Canadian Programs That Support Manufacturing	13
Table 2: German Programs That Support Manufacturing	17
Table 3: Japanese Programs That Support Manufacturing	22
Table 4: Overall Expenditure on Research and Development, for Five Selected Countries, 1999 and 2009	23
Table 5: South Korean Programs That Support Manufacturing	25
Table 6: Comparison of National Technical Support and Product Development Programs	28
Table 7: Comparison of Cluster Programs	30
Table 8: Comparison of Funding for R&D Grant Programs	31

Table 9: Number of Export Promotion Personnel and Number of
Countries where Export Promotion Activities Are
Conducted by Five Countries   33
Table 10: Export Promotion Budgets of Five Countries Relative to
GDP and Export Volume[a]   34

Figures

Figure 1: Percentage of U.S. Nonfarm Workers in Manufacturing,
1945-2012   4
Figure 2: U.S. Manufacturing Value-Added as a Percentage of Gross
Domestic Product, 1947-2012   5
Figure 3: Manufacturing Value Added for Selected Countries, 1998-
2010   6
Figure 4: Types of Potential Government Policies to Support
Innovation, Trade and Training   10
Figure 5: Foreign and U.S. Manufacturing Statistics   12
Figure 6: TIRI voltage testing room   65

Abbreviations

BLS	Bureau of Labor Statistics
CICP	Canadian Innovation Commercialization Program
Commerce	U.S. Department of Commerce
Daedeok	Daedeok Innopolis
Daejeon	Daejeon Technopark
ETRI	Electronics and Telecommunications Research Institute
GDP	Gross Domestic Product
IRAP	Industrial Research Assistance Program
JIAC	Jobs and Innovation Accelerator Challenge
KOTRA	Korea Trade-Investment Promotion Agency
Labor	U.S. Department of Labor
MEP	Hollings Manufacturing Extension Partnership
METI	Ministry of Economy, Trade, and Industry
NAMII	National Additive Manufacturing Innovation Institute
NEDO	New Energy and Industrial Technology Development Organization
NGV	Next Generation Vehicle
NIST	National Institute of Standards and Technology
NNMI	National Network for Manufacturing Innovation
OECD	Organisation for Economic Co-operation and Development
PCAST	President's Council of Advisors on Science & Technology
Perkins Act	Carl D. Perkins Career and Technical Education Improvement Act of 2006
R&D	Research and Development
SME	Small- and medium-sized enterprises
SR&ED	Scientific Research and Experimental Development
State	U.S. Department of State
TAMA	Technology Advanced Metropolitan Area
TIRI	Tokyo Metropolitan Industrial Technology Research Institute
TPP	Trans-Pacific Partnership
TPCC	Trade Promotion Coordinating Committee
USD	U. S. Dollars
WIA	Workforce Investment Act of 1998

July 25, 2013

The Honorable John D. Rockefeller IV
Chairman
Committee on Commerce, Science, & Transportation
United States Senate

Dear Mr. Chairman:

Even though certain measures show that the manufacturing sector in the United States remains competitive worldwide, over the last decade it has lost over one-third of its workforce. There are concerns that this decline in employment indicates a loss of international competitiveness as well as shrinking job opportunities for middle-class workers. Other developed economies have also faced manufacturing job losses and have had concerns about manufacturing competitiveness, particularly as China has claimed a rapidly increasing share of global manufacturing production. There may be important insights for the United States to glean from the manufacturing policies and strategies of similarly-situated countries, which are facing some of the same challenges of increased competition in manufacturing from developing countries. We were asked to identify innovative manufacturing programs from other countries that may help inform U.S. policy. Specifically, we examined the following questions:

1. What government strategies and programs have other advanced economies implemented to approach issues similar to those facing manufacturing in the United States?

2. What key distinctions exist between policy approaches to support manufacturing in other advanced economies and those in the United States?

To identify foreign countries and innovative manufacturing programs that may help inform U.S. manufacturing policy, we interviewed a range of manufacturing experts about key manufacturing issues and obtained their views about which foreign countries had innovative manufacturing programs. We selected four comparison countries to study—Canada, Germany, Japan, and South Korea—based on recommendations from experts, including U.S. officials from the Departments of Commerce (Commerce) and Labor (Labor), consideration of the countries' economic and political similarities to the United States, and information from our own research of foreign programs that support manufacturing. We then worked with officials from the U.S. Department of State (State) stationed in the selected four countries and foreign embassy officials to select specific programs for our review. We did not attempt to perform a comprehensive review of manufacturing programs in the four selected foreign countries, nor did we seek information in all countries about programs in each of our three key policy categories—innovation, trade, and training. To learn about our selected foreign programs, we met with foreign officials administering these programs and reviewed documents they provided.[1] To identify key distinctions between foreign and U.S. approaches to manufacturing, we researched comparable programs in the United States, selected in part based on suggestions from Commerce and Labor, and interviewed staff administering those programs. We did not attempt to do a comprehensive review of U.S. manufacturing programs, nor attempt to assess the effectiveness of any country's programs.

This report uses data obtained from large U.S. and international agencies and from foreign manufacturing agencies. We assessed the reliability of data from the Bureau of Labor Statistics (BLS), the Bureau of Economic Analysis, the World Bank, and the Organisation for Economic Co-operation and Development (OECD) by reviewing literature provided by the organizations regarding their methodology for compiling data, including measures to ensure data quality and comparability across countries. We determined that these data were sufficiently reliable for the purposes of our report. We did not independently attempt to confirm the reliability of data provided by foreign manufacturing agencies except where documentary evidence provided by those agencies allowed us to; we did confirm the accuracy of the figures and our use of them by having foreign officials review relevant excerpts of the report. We found these data to be sufficiently reliable for our purposes. For data on export promotion, we assessed the reliability of data from the World Trade Organization by reviewing literature provided by that organization regarding its methodology for compiling data, reviewed the methodology of an International Trade Administration study that compared and analyzed foreign countries' export promotion budget levels, and accessed the websites of Canadian, German, Japanese, and South Korean export promotion agencies to obtain the number of countries in which those

---

[1] We did not analyze or review foreign laws or regulations, and relied on program information, including budget information, from sources provided by foreign agency officials and other sources. Moreover, we did not evaluate the effectiveness of any foreign programs.

countries offered export promotion services; we found the data sufficiently reliable for our purposes. Appendix I contains additional information about our scope and methodology.

We conducted this performance audit from March 2012 to July 2013 in accordance with generally accepted government auditing standards. Those standards require that we plan and perform the audit to obtain sufficient, appropriate evidence to provide a reasonable basis for our findings and conclusions based on our audit objectives. We believe that the evidence obtained provides a reasonable basis for our findings and conclusions based on our audit objectives.

Background

The U.S. manufacturing sector comprises businesses that are engaged in the mechanical, physical, or chemical transformation of materials, substances, or components into new products, including sectors such as machinery, textiles, apparel, food production, and chemicals. However, U.S. policy makers have become focused on competing in high-end, or "advanced manufacturing." While no consensus definition of advanced manufacturing exists, it refers generally to the production of scientifically- and technologically-intensive products, in which the economic value derives from inputs of knowledge and design more than it reflects traditional inputs such as labor and materials.[2] Robotics, nanomanufacturing, and electric vehicles are examples of advanced manufacturing sub-industries.

U.S. Manufacturing Performance Statistics

Statistics present a mixed picture about the health of U.S. manufacturing, both relative to the rest of the U.S. economy and to other countries' manufacturing sectors. According to data from BLS, manufacturing employment has fallen from 17.6 million workers in 1998 to 11.5 million in early 2010, a decline of over one-third over a period in which total U.S. employment grew somewhat. However, the decline in U.S. manufacturing employment is not a new phenomenon, and a longer-term view shows a steady decline of manufacturing's share of all American jobs. As figure 1

---

[2] The President's Council of Advisers on Science and Technology describes it as "a family of activities that (a) depend on the use and coordination of information, automation, computation, software, sensing, and networking, and/or (b) make use of cutting edge materials and emerging capabilities enabled by the physical and biological sciences." See Executive Office of the President, President's Council of Advisers on Science and Technology, *Report to the President on Ensuring American Leadership in Advanced Manufacturing* (Washington, D.C.: June 2011).

shows, the percentage of U.S. nonfarm workers in manufacturing has dropped steadily since the end of World War II, from about 35 percent in 1945 to about 9 percent in 2012. Since bottoming out in 2010, manufacturing employment rebounded slowly up to about 12 million workers at the end of 2012. Also, other advanced economies, such as Canada, Germany, Japan, and the United Kingdom, suffered large manufacturing job losses from 1998 to 2011, suggesting that global economic forces have affected manufacturing employment in addition to any factors that may be unique to the United States.

Figure 1: Percentage of U.S. Nonfarm Workers in Manufacturing, 1945-2012

Percentage of U.S. nonfarm workers employed in manufacturing

Source: GAO analysis of Bureau of Labor Statistics data.

Similar to the employment trend, manufacturing has accounted for a decreasing share of U.S. economic output over the last several decades, from about 28 percent of U.S. gross domestic product (GDP) in the early 1950's to a recent low of 11 percent in 2009 (see fig. 2).

GAO-13-365 Global Manufacturing

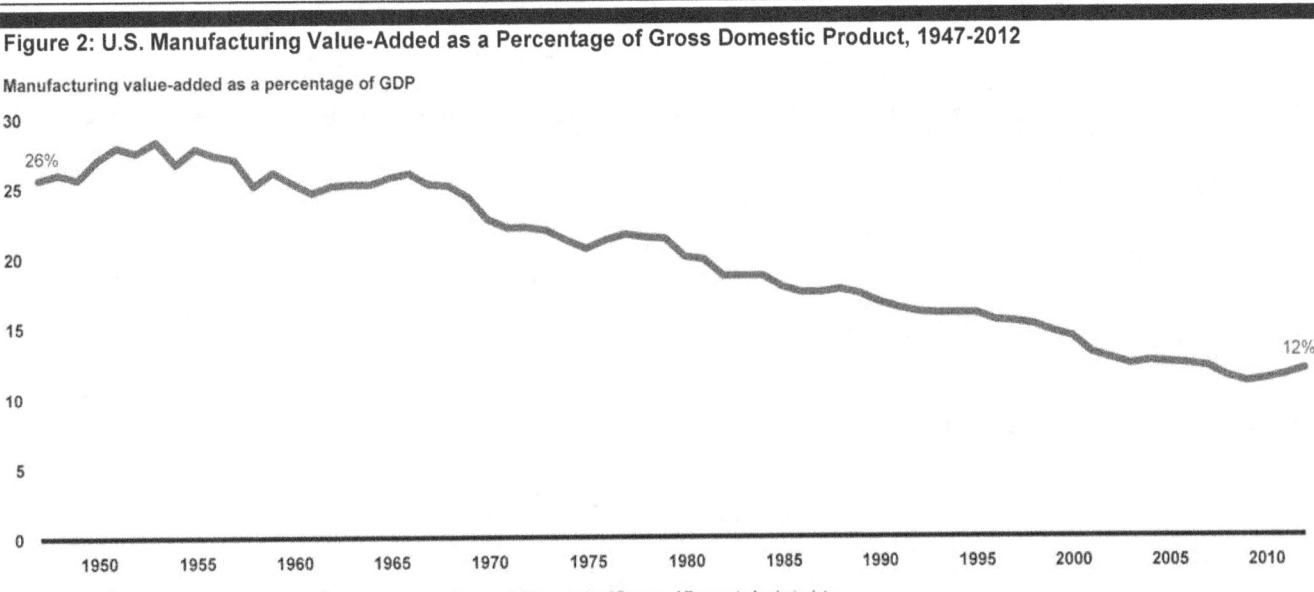

Figure 2: U.S. Manufacturing Value-Added as a Percentage of Gross Domestic Product, 1947-2012

Source: GAO analysis of Bureau of Economic Analysis data.

Moreover, the decrease in manufacturing's share of employment and GDP could reflect increasing worker productivity in manufacturing and the emergence and growth of other U.S. industries. According to data from BLS, U.S. manufacturing productivity, measured as output per hour, rose 55.7 percent from 2002 to 2011, exceeded only by the Czech Republic, South Korea, Singapore, and Taiwan among 19 measured countries. Furthermore, after contracting in 2008 and 2009, manufacturing contributed more to the percent change in U.S. GDP than any other industry group in 2010 and 2012, as well as playing a leading role in somewhat weaker GDP growth in 2011.

When compared to the manufacturing sectors in other countries, some statistics show that the United States performs well. Figure 3 shows the change in manufacturing value-added for Canada, China, Germany, Japan, South Korea, and the United States from 1998 to 2010, in constant year 2000 U.S. dollars.[3] The figure shows that China and South Korea have experienced a rapid increase in manufacturing production

---

[3] Value-added is a measure of output after accounting for intermediate inputs used in production.

GAO-13-365 Global Manufacturing

over this period, while U.S. manufacturing value-added has grown about as fast as that in Japan, Germany, and Canada.[4]

Figure 3: Manufacturing Value Added for Selected Countries, 1998-2010

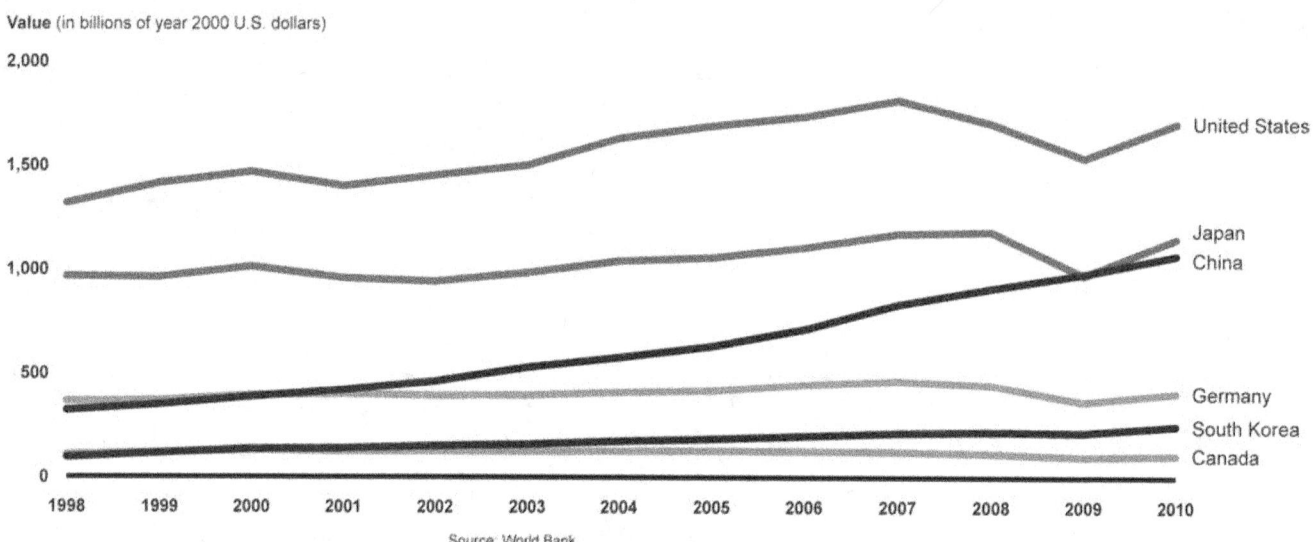

Value (in billions of year 2000 U.S. dollars)

Source: World Bank.

Some manufacturing experts, however, maintain that official statistics misrepresent the state of U.S. manufacturing because productivity and value-added statistics do not properly account for the value of imported inputs in goods manufactured in the United States. As these imports become cheaper, or as manufacturers shift to lower-cost imported inputs, the value-added of the resulting manufactured good rises, suggesting more manufacturing "production," even though nothing meaningful may have changed about manufacturing competitiveness.[5] The Information Technology and Innovation Foundation, an innovation policy think tank,

---

[4] According to the U.S.-China Economic and Security Review Commission, official Chinese statistics on national output suffer from deficiencies that detract from their reliability, but we believe that the reported data are sufficient for the illustrative purposes we intend here.

[5] For more information on how imports potentially affect productivity and value-added, see Susan Houseman, Christopher Kurz, Paul Lengermann, and Benjamin Mandel, "Offshoring Bias in U.S. Manufacturing," *Journal of Economic Perspectives.* Vol. 25, No. 2 (Spring 2011).

estimated in a 2012 report that official statistics overstate productivity growth from 2000-2010 by 122 percent.[6]

Key Policy Areas Related to Manufacturing

Not all experts agree on what role, if any, the government should play in supporting manufacturing. Economic theory generally suggests that government intervention into private sector activity is justified by "market failure"—situations in which the private market under- or over-produces a good because private interests differ from society's. Those supportive of enhancing productivity in manufacturing suggest that government policy should target the sector in order to remedy market failures that may hinder innovation—the development and application of new knowledge. Innovation underpins improvements in the way capital and labor are combined to create new products and increase productivity. This makes it critical for the broader economy and particularly important for manufacturing.

An important element of innovation is research and development (R&D), the testing and application of new ideas. R&D is seen as a key source of innovation and its application to new products and technologies. The private sector, however, faces disincentives to investing in R&D— it may be expensive, it often fails, willing firms may lack sufficient finances, and successful R&D may produce benefits that the investing firm cannot capture — leading to possible underinvestment in R&D and underproduction in innovation without government support. These disincentives may be particularly difficult to overcome for small- and medium-sized enterprises (SME). Though innovation policy can address market failure across all sectors of the economy, advocates of targeted innovation policy argue that it may provide particular benefit to manufacturing. They note that the sector depends on continually creating new ideas for products and ways to make those products. They also observe that manufacturing is a significant source of R&D; according to the National Science Foundation, the sector accounted for 70 percent of private-sector spending on R&D in the United States in 2008.

In practical terms, to support needed innovation, the government may intervene through various policies, some of which may have a focus on the manufacturing sector.[7] These include:

---

[6] Robert D. Atkinson, Luke A. Stewart, Scott M. Andes, and Stephen J. Ezell, "Worse Than the Great Depression," The Information Technology & Innovation Foundation (Washington, D.C., March 2012).

- Public support for "basic" R&D in science and engineering, which, while conducted without specific commercial applications in mind, can spur private-sector innovation. The public sector may be well-suited to conducting basic R&D directly, through government scientific agencies, public universities, and other research institutions, because it is unlikely that most private firms would conduct this type of general research without a potentially profitable application in mind.
- Public support for private-sector "applied" R&D, research that seeks to solve practical problems or develop new products and commercialization. Applied R&D is seen as a key component in helping innovators overcome the so-called "valley of death", the difficult transition between new ideas and commercially viable manufacturing products or processes. Support for applied R&D could take various forms:

  - Subsidies for private investment in R&D, through direct funding or tax incentives, and assistance with financing for private R&D projects with commercialization potential, which may overcome the difficulty some firms may face in obtaining funding from private financial markets. However, it may be difficult for the government to figure out which firms merit subsidy because of the lack of information or foresight into an individual firm's growth prospects.
  - Public infrastructure investment that facilitates R&D and knowledge transfer, such as research laboratories, transportation investment, and "knowledge" infrastructure such as broadband telecommunications, the development of measurement techniques and databases, and the dissemination of technical expertise. Experts have referred to such widely-accessible infrastructure or knowledge as the "industrial commons" that provides a base for innovation and production, and see investment in these commons as an important source of new ideas for products or processes and solutions to existing problems.
  - Public support for innovation clusters — regional concentrations of large and small companies that develop creative products and services, along with specialized suppliers, service providers, universities, and associated institutions. Firms in a cluster may be able to share knowledge and transact business at lower cost than if they were far apart, possibly leading to increased innovation.[8]

---

[7] The listed policies are not intended to be exhaustive, nor are we recommending or endorsing the adoption of any particular policy option or set of options.

[8] See, for example, Michael E. Porter, "Clusters of Innovation: Regional Foundations of U.S. Competitiveness," Council on Competitiveness (Washington, D.C.: October 2001).

However, the effectiveness of cluster policy has not been established; the formation of successful clusters in the United States, such as California's Silicon Valley, suggests that government support for clusters may not be necessary.

Government support for manufacturing can also involve other efforts that support activities that may suffer from market failures:

- Development of knowledge and workforce skills. Like investment in R&D, private firms may lack the incentive to invest in worker training because the firms may not recoup a sufficient investment if workers take their training to another firm or if skills become obsolete. As manufacturing has become more technologically advanced, various experts have highlighted the increased importance of skills training in advanced manufacturing, as well as the adaptability of workers and training resources. Manufacturing in scientifically-intensive fields will also require a pipeline of workers with advanced degrees in science, technology, engineering, and mathematics. A recent study from the Brookings Institution uses the Bureau of Labor Statistics' data to project that nearly half of all job openings in the U.S. economy over the next decade will be for "middle-skill" jobs, those requiring more than high school but less than a college degree.[9]

- Promotion of open trade and global competition, through trade liberalization, the provision of information, advice, and advocacy for exporters (referred to as export promotion), the protection of intellectual property rights, development and harmonization of international technological standards, and the enforcement of trade rules. While free trade agreements have decreased the significance of tariffs as a trade barrier, some experts have argued that non-tariff barriers have become increasingly problematic. These could include restrictive technical standards, packaging, and local content requirements, among others.[10] Trade policy may be especially critical for manufacturing since the sector may play a key role in restoring a healthy balance of trade. In 2012, Commerce reported that in 2010,

---

[9] Harry J. Holzer, and Robert I. Lerman, "The Future of Middle-Skill Jobs," CCF Brief #41 (Washington, D.C.: Brookings Institution, February 2009).

[10] For more on nontariff barriers, see GAO, *Export-Import Bank, Reaching New Targets for Environmentally Beneficial Exports Presents Major Challenges for Bank*, GAO-10-682 (Washington, D.C.: July 14, 2010); and *International Trade: Four Free Trade Agreements GAO Reviewed Have Resulted in Commercial Benefits, but Challenges on Labor and Environment Remain*, GAO-09-439 (Washington, D.C.: July 2009).

manufactured goods represented 86 percent of all U.S. goods exported and 60 percent of total U.S. exports.[11]

Figure 4 provides a summary of some key types of support that governments can provide to support innovation, training, and trade, which can benefit manufacturing and other sectors.

Figure 4: Types of Potential Government Policies to Support Innovation, Trade and Training

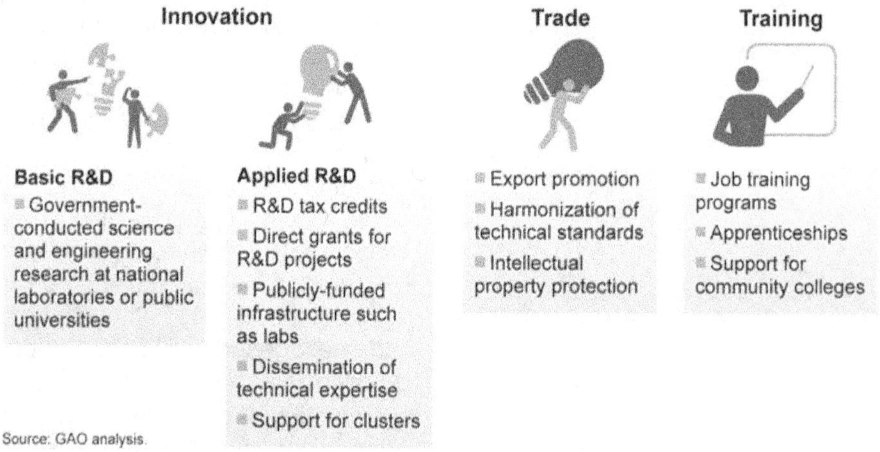

Source: GAO analysis.

Note: The listed policies are not intended to be exhaustive, nor are we recommending or endorsing the adoption of any particular policy option or set of options.

Administration of Manufacturing Policy in the United States

In the United States, the federal government has generally taken the lead in supporting basic research, providing the economic framework, and constructing infrastructure. Commerce administers manufacturing programs through sub-agencies such as the National Institute of Standards and Technology (NIST), the Economic Development Administration (EDA), and the International Trade Administration. Other U.S. agencies support manufacturing as part of their program activities, including the Department of Defense, the Department of Energy, National Aeronautics and Space Administration, and the National Science Foundation. Labor administers training programs for job seekers through the Employment and Training Administration. In addition, tax breaks such as the R&D tax credit further benefit manufacturers (although these

---

[11] See U.S. Department of Commerce, *The Competitiveness and Innovative Capacity of the United States* (Washington D.C.: January 2012).

provisions do not apply exclusively to manufacturers). States and localities have the main responsibility for education and also are most active in promoting regional economic development, including measures that support innovation. See appendix II for more information on recent U.S. manufacturing initiatives.

Other Economically Advanced Countries Have Instituted a Varied Mix of Programs to Address Key Manufacturing Issues in Their Countries

The four countries we analyzed—Canada, Germany, Japan, and South Korea—take varied approaches to government support for manufacturing, with each providing a different mix of programs to support their manufacturing sectors.[12] For example, Canada has started directly supporting SMEs to encourage innovation. Germany has created programs for innovation and maintained long-standing programs to support export promotion and skills training. Recently, Japan's manufacturing policies have emphasized alternative energy and the production and innovation that come from that sector. Japan also prioritizes providing hands-on assistance to SMEs. South Korea has substantially expanded investments in R&D to strengthen its manufacturing sector. Figure 5 presents key manufacturing statistics for each of these countries and the United States.

---

[12] We did not independently evaluate these programs, or analyze or review any foreign laws or regulations. To obtain specific program information, we interviewed foreign officials overseeing each program and relied on program information from sources provided by these foreign officials and other sources.

Figure 5: Foreign and U.S. Manufacturing Statistics

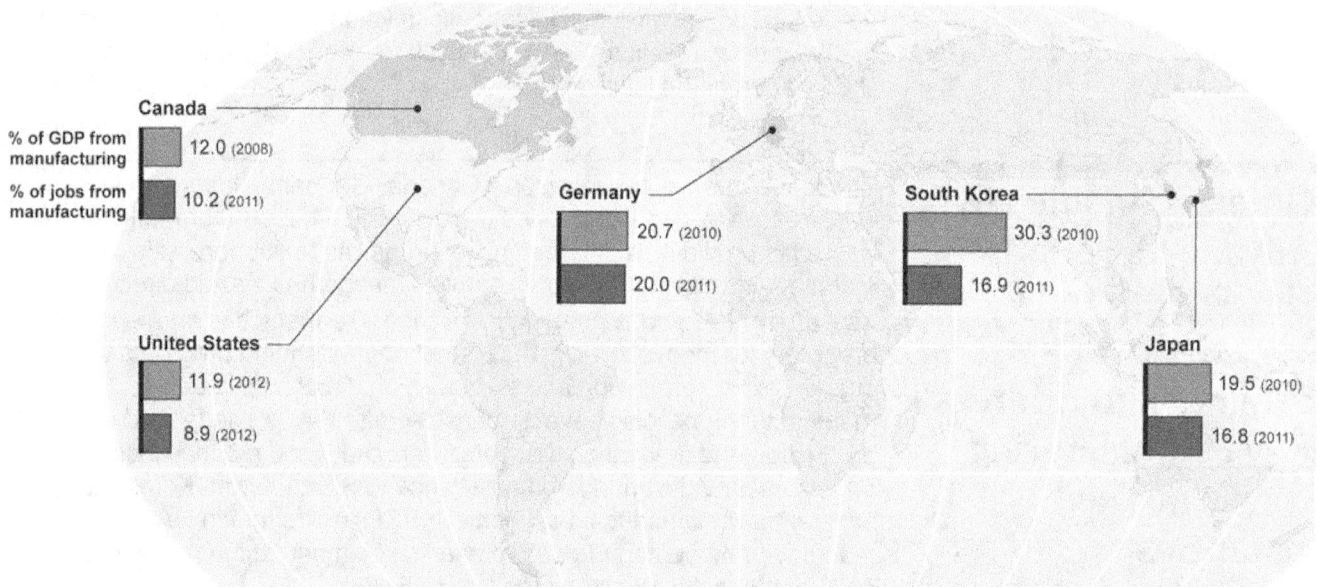

Canada
% of GDP from manufacturing
12.0 (2008)
% of jobs from manufacturing
10.2 (2011)

Germany
20.7 (2010)
20.0 (2011)

South Korea
30.3 (2010)
16.9 (2011)

United States
11.9 (2012)
8.9 (2012)

Japan
19.5 (2010)
16.8 (2011)

Source: Bureau of Labor Statistics (employment); World Bank (Canada, Germany, Japan, South Korea percentage of GDP); Bureau of Economic Analysis (United States manufacturing output); National Atlas of the United States (base map).

Canada Is Shifting Emphasis from Tax Policy to Direct Support for Small and Medium Enterprises to Encourage Innovation

Recent trends in the Canadian economy, including the rising value of the Canadian dollar to near parity with the U.S. dollar and declining productivity growth, have put pressure on Canada's manufacturing sector. In 2010, according to the Canadian government, Canada continued to lag behind other advanced economies in terms of business innovation performance despite a high level of federal support for R&D. In response, Canada's 2010 budget called for a comprehensive review of all federal support for R&D. The resulting report—commonly referred to as the Jenkins report—catalogued a set of 60 R&D programs worth about $5 billion Canadian in fiscal year 2010-2011. The Jenkins report found that Canada's support for business innovation was heavily weighted toward the Scientific Research and Experimental Development (SR&ED) tax credit, but that the calculation of some SR&ED expenses was highly complex, which resulted in excessive compliance costs for SMEs in particular. The report also found that other countries relied less than Canada on indirect tax incentives to stimulate innovation, and that Canadian federal policy should provide more effective support to innovative firms, particularly SMEs, to help them grow and become competitive. To address these findings, the Jenkins report recommended simplifying the SR&ED and redeploying the savings from this toward more direct support to SMEs in order to encourage innovation. To further expand opportunities for innovation in Canada, the Jenkins report also recommended that the government provide innovative firms with more access to venture capital, and make better use of government procurement by leveraging the government's substantial purchasing power to create demand for leading-edge goods, services, and technologies from Canadian enterprises.

Canada's 2012 national budget, in turn, contained several changes that acted on the Jenkins report recommendations. According to Canadian budget documents, effective 2014, the SR&ED tax credit will be reduced; the budget of the Industrial Research and Assistance Program, which employs a national network of technical advisors who work directly with SMEs to help them grow through the commercialization of innovative products and services, was increased. The 2012 budget also announced a new $400 million venture capital fund to support innovative start-up firms. To address the report's recommendation on procurement, the Canadian Innovation Commercialization Program was made permanent in order to assist SMEs in doing business with the government of Canada.

Table 1 highlights examples of manufacturing-related programs in Canada. For further information on Canadian programs included in this review, see Appendix III.

Table 1: Canadian Programs That Support Manufacturing

Program/initiative	Program/initiative description	2012 budget (in USD millions)	Year founded/ introduced
Innovation			
Canadian Innovation Commercialization Program	Provides assistance with the commercialization of new goods and services.	95, over 3 years; 40 annually thereafter[a]	2010
Industrial Research Assistance Program	A network of expert advisors who assist small- and medium-sized enterprises with innovation efforts.	258[b]	1965
Scientific Research and Experimental Development tax incentives	Federal tax incentives to stimulate research and development activities.	3,604[c]	1994[d]
Venture Capital Action Plan	A federally-funded program that aims to increase private-sector investment in early-stage risk-capital and to support the creation of large-scale venture capital funds led by the private sector.	400	2012
Training			
Red Seal Program	An apprenticeship program that provides a national definition of competency in 55 trades.	No information available[e]	1952[f]

Source: GAO analysis of Industry Canada, Finance Canada, the National Research Council, Human Resources and Skills Development Canada documents, and Canada's Economic Action Plan 2012.

Note: Amounts converted to U.S. dollars from Canadian dollars and rounded to the nearest million.

^aThis funding was available starting in 2013.

^bAmount includes additional $90 million in funding provided to Industrial Research Assistance Program through the 2012 budget.

^cAccording to Finance Canada officials, this amount represents an estimate of the tax expenditure associated with the Scientific Research and Experimental Development tax incentive program for the year 2012.

^dAccording to Canadian officials, tax credits to encourage research and development were first established in 1944 and were subject to several major revisions over the years. The Scientific Research and Experimental Development tax incentive program in its current form was implemented in 1994.

^eThe Red Seal Program has federal, provincial, and territorial sources of support. We were unable to obtain information on the total budget for the program.

^fThe Red Seal Program was established in the early 1950s following the first national conference on Apprenticeship in Trades and Industry in 1952. The 1952 conference produced an agreement to develop national standards in the form of National Occupational Analyses, and was followed shortly after by an interprovincial examination program for certifying tradespersons, thus initiating Canada's move toward national standards in trades training.

Germany Has Established New Programs in Innovation to Complement Long-Standing Trade and Training Programs

Despite slow economic growth at the turn of the century and contraction in 2008-2009, the German economy has grown steadily over recent years. According to German officials, this growth has been in part a result of the strength of Germany's manufacturing sector, which accounts for about 22 percent of GDP. German officials told us that after the recession of 2008-2009, manufacturing recovered relatively quickly in part because of an arrangement between unions, employers, and the government through which (1) employers reduced their employees' hours to avoid layoffs, and (2) the government subsidized a portion of employees' lost salaries. According to German officials, this arrangement allowed businesses to continue to operate through the economic downturn, and then expand workers' hours once the economy recovered. A 2012 OECD report estimates that the agreement may have prevented up to 500,000 layoffs.[13]

To make the most of existing growth potential and open new prospects for German industry, the German government issued its High Tech Strategy 2020 in 2006. The strategy guides the specific efforts across national government agencies and programs. Specifically, it states that in order for Germany to become a leader in solving global challenges, the government will need to stimulate R&D in five priority areas: (1) climate and energy, (2) health and nutrition, (3) mobility, (4) security, and (5)

---

[13] OECD (2012), *OECD Economic Surveys: Germany 2012* (OECD Publishing). http://dx.doi.org/10.1787/eco_surveys-deu-2012-en. Accessed March 18, 2013.

communication. The German government has, in turn, recently established several programs to promote innovation in these areas.

The High Tech Strategy 2020 provides a framework for recent programs that encourage applied research and innovation, particularly in SMEs, and also for a program that supports business clusters that conduct R&D in the strategy's five priority areas. According to German officials, SMEs are a significant part of the German economy and have long played a role in German manufacturing.[14] However, the national government has identified innovation as a challenge across the SME sector. In response, according to German officials and German government documents, the German government has in recent years initiated a group of programs intended to strengthen innovation in SMEs. These programs—all initiated in 2006 or later—include the following:

- The Central Innovation Program for SMEs, which is Germany's largest program to support innovation in SMEs, provides grant funding to pursue innovative ideas that show high potential for commercialization.
- The HighTech Grunderfonds program is a public-private venture capital fund that invests in innovative start-up companies.
- Signo provides federal assistance to SMEs in securing intellectual property for innovative products and helps SMEs file for patents with the German Patent and Trademark Office.

According to German officials and German government documents, as part of its High Tech Strategy, Germany also established the Spitzencluster program to continue the national emphasis on innovation by funding business clusters judged through a competitive application process to be the best, or "leading edge" clusters in the country.

In addition to these more recent programs, according to representatives of Germany's Fraunhofer Institutes, skilled Fraunhofer researchers pursue joint applied R&D projects with businesses that result in commercializable processes and products. Germany established the Fraunhofer Institutes, a nationwide network of 60 applied research facilities with research expert staff, in 1949 as part of efforts to rebuild its research infrastructure after World War II, according to Fraunhofer

---

[14] According to Germany's Ministry of Economy and Technology, the German government defines SMEs as businesses of 500 or fewer employees and up to €50 million in revenue.

officials. Fraunhofer's applied research projects include the following categories of specialization: (1) materials and components, (2) microelectronics, (3) information and communications technology, (4) production, (5) light and surfaces, and (6) life sciences. Fraunhofer officials told us that Fraunhofer Institutes are co-located with universities, which allows companies access to skilled researchers.

In contrast to Germany's newer programs to support innovation, Germany's main national system to support the export of manufactured goods has a much longer history of providing support to the manufacturing sector. According to German officials, Germany is a leading exporter of manufactured technology goods. German officials also told us that Germany's long-established export promotion organization, the Association of Chambers of Commerce and Industry, brings together an agency of the national government and all exporting businesses to share export information.[15] Germany fosters export activities in two main ways: (1) by selectively establishing partnerships abroad, and (2) by providing assistance for trade fair attendance and participation in trade delegations.

In addition to programs in innovation and trade, Germany also maintains a dual training system, which was established in law in 1970 but has existed in practice for centuries, according to German officials. German officials explained that the dual training system—through which German high school-age students complete apprenticeships in skilled trades—is a cooperative effort among business, labor, federal and state government representatives, coordinated by the Federal Institute for Vocational Education and Training. The Federal Institute for Vocational Education and Training, an institute of the national government, is responsible for regularly incorporating stakeholder feedback into the process of creating and updating skills certification standards. The executive board of the Federal Institute for Vocational Education and Training includes representatives from German unions, employers' associations, federal agencies, and state governments. Because of this role in bringing together stakeholders in the skills education process, the Federal Institute for Vocational Education and Training is often referred to as the "parliament" of vocational education in Germany.

---

[15] According to the German Association of Chambers of Commerce and Industry, German businesses are required to belong to their local chapter of the Chambers of Commerce and Industry, resulting in a national network of exporting businesses.

Table 2 highlights examples of manufacturing-related programs in Germany. For further information on German programs included in this review, see Appendix III.

Table 2: German Programs That Support Manufacturing

Program/initiative	Program/initiative Description	2012 budget (in USD millions)	Year founded/ introduced
Innovation			
Fraunhofer Institutes	A network of 60 applied research institutes nationwide; each institute specializes in a particular topic (e.g., factory automation, transportation and infrastructure systems, silicon technology)	2,800[a]	1949
Spitzencluster	A competitive national program that selects the best or 'leading edge' of Germany's many industrial clusters. Clusters selected as part of Spitzencluster receive some federal support	Spitzencluster awarded up to $51 million each to 5 clusters, for a total of $257 million. The awards are provided over 5 years	2007
Central Innovation Program for SMEs	Provides grants and low-interest loans to small and medium enterprises (SMEs) to help finance research and innovation projects. The program connects SMEs with technical advisors that guide the process of developing innovative projects.	643	2007
HighTech Grunderfonds	HighTech Grunderfonds provides support for high-tech start-up businesses.	411	2007
Signo	Provides federal assistance to small- and medium-sized enterprises to help with filing patent applications.	22	2006
Trade			
Association of Chambers of Commerce and Industry	A national network of 80 local chambers of commerce that coordinates Germany's export promotion activities and plays a role in the dual training system.	219	1872
Training			
Federal Institute for Vocational Education and Training: Dual training system (apprenticeships)	The dual training system combines classroom instruction with on-the-job training to provide apprenticeships for secondary school-age students who wish to pursue a skilled trade instead of university education. A variety of national, state, and private sector actors participate in the funding and management of the system.	50[b]	1970[c]

Source: GAO analysis of Fraunhofer Network, Federal Ministry of Education and Research, Federal Ministry of Economy and Technology, Association of Chambers of Commerce and Industry, Federal Institute for Vocational Education and Training documents.

Note: Amounts have been converted to U.S. dollars from euros and rounded to the nearest million.

[a]Officials from Germany's Federal Ministry of Education and Research told us their agency contributes about $595 million to the Fraunhofer budget annually. Fraunhofer Institutes also receive funding from other public sources, and generate revenue through research contracts with private companies.

[b]Other costs of the dual training system are covered by the Federal Ministry for Labor and Social Affairs, private businesses, and state governments.

Japan Has Used Energy Issues to Reshape its Manufacturing Policy

After two decades of economic stagnation and fallout from the 2011 Fukushima earthquake and nuclear disaster, Japan has made efforts to strengthen its economy—including its manufacturing sector—and improve its global competitiveness. Japan's manufacturing sector has been recognized in the past for its ability to make incremental improvements to manufactured products—for example, small just-in-time improvements made specifically for a subsequent phase of the manufacturing process—illustrated by the often-copied lean manufacturing practices that a well-known automobile manufacturer developed over several decades.[16]

Officials from Ministry of Economy, Trade, and Industry (METI), the country's main ministry for manufacturing policy, identified genbaryoku—capabilities to find and solve problems in the field—as a unique source of strength in Japan's manufacturing industry. According to these officials, this capability helped Japan to restore its economy quickly after damage from the earthquake. In the wake of the 2011 Fukushima crisis, many SMEs went out of business, and global companies, including automobile manufacturers, faced delays in delivery of inputs and in production, according to Japanese officials. As a result, METI officials said that the Japanese government and automobile industry started working to establish more diverse and reliable supply networks.[17]

---

[16] Lean manufacturing is a management philosophy derived mostly from the Toyota Production System. A lean organization understands customer value and focuses its key processes to continuously increase it. The ultimate goal is to provide perfect value to the customer through a perfect value creation process that has zero waste.

[17] Going forward, the Trans-Pacific Partnership (TPP) agreement will influence the ways in which the United States and other countries structure trade policies to support manufacturing. The TPP will provide a regulatory framework intended to increase regional trade integration by establishing agreements in areas such as regulatory coherence, customs, financial services, labor, intellectual property, and market access. Round 18 of negotiations is currently set to take place in July 2013. Japan has announced its intent to join the ongoing TPP talks. With respect to trade in manufactured goods in the region, the TPP agreement will potentially affect the Japanese, U.S., and Canadian auto sectors by providing ways to harmonize standards and manage the region's integrated auto supply chains. Japanese officials told us that the automotive sector is an important part of its manufacturing sector and accounts for significant portions of its manufacturing-related employment and production.

In 2007, the Japanese government published a comprehensive innovation plan: the "Innovation 25" initiative, a long-term strategy for innovation in engineering, information technology, and other fields by the year 2025. This initiative established a cabinet-level minister for innovation and called for several new policies, including: 1) reviewing regulations to establish an environment that supports innovation, (2) promoting the use of new technologies in the public sector, and (3) strengthening activities for international standardization. According to the Center for Strategic and International Studies, this plan introduced the concept of an innovation "ecosystem" in Japan, which emphasizes collaboration among universities, research institutes, the private sector, and government—similar to clusters—rather than the private sector acting alone to develop and commercialize innovations.

Japan developed its most recent 5-year Science and Technology Basic Plan in 2011.[18] This plan is aimed at reconstruction and revival from the Fukushima disaster and realizing sustainable growth, for example, by focusing on green innovation. The goal of this Basic Plan is to provide a concrete plan for implementing Japan's comprehensive New Growth Strategy introduced in the same year. As an outgrowth of the third science and technology plan, the Japanese government initiated several regional innovation cluster programs to enhance Japan's competitiveness. One of these programs, the Industrial Cluster Project, is composed of groups of local SMEs and venture businesses that use research obtained from universities and other institutions. One of 18 such clusters in Japan—the Technology Advanced Metropolitan Area (TAMA) Association—has over 600 entities, including universities, financial institutions, local governments, businesses, and industry groups, according to one TAMA Association official. The TAMA Association supports local SME manufacturers by matching them with larger businesses that have complementary needs at the national, regional, and local levels to improve R&D and commercialization of technology and products. For example, the TAMA Association connects manufacturers in

---

[18] According to Japanese government documents, Japan developed the first of these plans in 1996 to set guidelines for the comprehensive and systematic implementation of Japan's overall science and technology promotion policy. One goal of this first basic plan was to double government spending on R&D. The second Basic Plan aimed to double the competitive funding through the end of 2005. The third Basic Plan, developed in 2006, focused on advancing innovation by promoting R&D in the private sector and the formation of regional clusters, and—similar to the Innovation 25 initiative—by promoting the use of new technologies in the public sector.

need of a particular type of R&D to university researchers with projects in that field.

In response to the 2011 Fukushima nuclear disaster, Japan has intertwined energy issues—especially alternative energy projects—in its manufacturing policy. The national government has laid out detailed alternative energy policies through its 2011 and 2012 comprehensive Rebirth of Japan strategies.[19] Among other things, the 2011 strategy outlines support for: (1) adopting renewable energies; (2) developing R&D hubs consisting of universities, research institutions, and private firms for industrial development and job creation purposes; and (3) adopting electric, heat, and other energy supply systems that make use of regional resources. The 2012 strategy outlines increased R&D for creating innovative green parts and materials, developing green vehicles, and improving battery performance. METI established the Next Generation Vehicle (NGV) Program, a key alternative energy initiative. According to METI officials, NGV's strategy takes an integrated approach involving six components: (1) development and production of the vehicles; (2) battery R&D and technology; (3) rare metal and resource recycling systems; (4) installation and infrastructure of chargers; (5) vehicle systems; and (6) international standards for battery performance and safety evaluation methods—and associated roadmaps. According to METI officials, NGV identifies diffusion targets for alternative-fuel vehicles and the development of related technologies.[20] For example, one of its goals is to develop advanced batteries for automobiles that will also have other uses, such as powering homes. As part of the NGV Program, Japan's government, in conjunction with industrial leaders, seeks to influence international technological standards for related manufacturing accessories, including battery performance and chargers, for which various countries are developing competing models.[21] The government also funds alternative energy projects, as well as other R&D intensive

---

[19] Japan developed the Rebirth of Japan strategy in 2011, updated in 2012. As part of this plan, Japan prioritized four key policy areas, including green energy and SMEs, providing the framework for about 40 initiatives and strategies to promote Japan as a technology and innovation leader.

[20] Japan's Agency for Natural Resources and Energy and the private sector also contributed to the development of the NGV Program.

[21] According to Japanese government and industry officials, there are competing technologies for quick battery chargers worldwide, which can charge electric vehicles up to 80 percent charge in 30 minutes—each with a separate nozzle for the charger plug.

GAO-13-365 Global Manufacturing

private-sector projects with commercial potential, through the New Energy and Industrial Technology Development Organization (NEDO). According to NEDO officials, NEDO connects university researchers and industry to collaborate on joint research, such as R&D in support of batteries and hydrogen fuel cells for electric vehicles.

The Rebirth of Japan strategies also include significant support for strengthening SMEs. For example, the 2011 strategy outlines overcoming the "valley of death"—the gap between innovative ideas and commercializable production—by promoting cooperation between industry, academia, and the government; encouraging joint R&D projects; and supporting overseas business for SMEs. The government also encourages SME technological innovation by offering technical and business support through a national network of Public Industrial Technology Research Institutes—known as Kohsetsushi centers. According to Japanese officials, these centers provide SME manufacturers with a range of services including technology guidance; technical assistance and training; networking; testing, analysis, and instrumentation; and access to open laboratories and test beds, and they typically offer technical consultation services free of charge. Kohsetsushi Centers support Japanese SME manufacturers in adopting emerging technologies, including nanotechnology and robotics. For example, the Tokyo Metropolitan Industrial Technology Research Institute (TIRI) serves about a quarter of Tokyo's 40,000 manufacturers across three locations, primarily by providing services, information, and testing equipment and facilities to SMEs, according to TIRI officials.

In addition, the Kawasaki Business Incubation Center rents offices and lab space to SMEs and entrepreneurs and provides some free services, such as introductions to potential partners and funding entities and support for completing applications for government subsidies or loans and establishing a registered corporation, according to Kawasaki Business Incubation Center officials. The center is located in close proximity to a number of larger companies and research institutes, which incubation officials told us helps facilitate collaboration. The center also provides training sessions on topics including machine operation to help companies acquire necessary technical skills. Having these resources nearby helps companies to move from basic R&D to practical applications in commercial products, and eventually to mass production since many of the tools needed for designing and manufacturing are in one place, according to Kawasaki City officials.

Table 3 highlights examples of manufacturing-related programs in Japan. For further information on Japanese programs included in this review, see Appendix III.

Table 3: Japanese Programs That Support Manufacturing

Program/ initiative	Program/ initiative description	Budget (in USD millions, fiscal year 2012)	Year founded/ introduced
Innovation			
Kawasaki Business Incubation Center	A center that rents office and lab space for companies as a venue for collaboration between companies.	1.4[a]	2003
Next Generation Vehicle Program	A comprehensive action plan for supporting research for next-generation cars, including battery technology, infrastructure (building and locating chargers), vehicle systems, and international standards.	434.8[b]	2010
New Energy and Industrial Technology Development Organization	An organization that promotes and manages R&D of energy, environment, and industrial technologies.	1,637.6	1980
Kohsetsushi Centers/ Tokyo Metropolitan Industrial Technology Research Institute	Centers that provide Japanese small- and medium-sized manufacturers with a range of services including technology guidance; technical assistance and training; networking; testing, analysis, and instrumentation; and access to open laboratories and test beds, among others.	2140/ 78.9	1902[c] / 2006[d]
Technology Advanced Metropolitan Area Association	A regional cluster that seeks to match large manufacturers, small- and medium-sized enterprises, universities, local governments, and financial institutions to improve R&D and commercialization of technology and products.	2.8	1998

Source: GAO analysis of Kawasaki Business Incubation Center; Next Generation Vehicle Program; New Energy and Industrial Technology Development Organization; Tokyo Metropolitan Industrial Technology Research Institute; Technology Advanced Metropolitan Area Association documents.

Note: Amounts converted to U.S. dollars from Japanese yen and rounded to the nearest million.

[a]Budget data as of 2011.

[b]According to the Ministry of Economy, Trade, and Industry officials, the agency is planning to spend almost $1 billion between fiscal years 2009 and 2016 on battery development, infrastructure installation, and subsidies.

[c]Refers to Kohsetsushi Centers.

[d]The Tokyo Metropolitan Industrial Technology Research Institute has existed in its present form since 2006, although it dates back at least to the early 1920s.

South Korea Has Substantially Expanded Investment in Research and Development to Strengthen Its Manufacturing Sector

Within the last 50 years, South Korea has shifted from receiving U.S. development assistance to becoming an OECD aid donor to other countries. According to the United States Agency for International Development, it is the only country to make this shift to date. Between 1999 and 2011, South Korean manufacturing output (in current U.S. dollars) has almost tripled. This rise has coincided with an increase in its investment in R&D, from approximately 2.2 percent of GDP in 1999 to approximately 3.4 percent in 2008, according to OECD statistics. As table 4 shows, South Korea's percentage increase in R&D spending over this period exceeded that of the other countries in our study, and as of 2009, South Korea spent more on R&D as a percentage of GDP than the other countries.[22]

Table 4: Overall Expenditure on Research and Development, for Five Selected Countries, 1999 and 2009

	Overall R&D expenditure (percent of GDP)		Change in overall (public and private) R&D expenditures (percent of GDP)
	1999	**2009**	
United States	2.64	2.79[a]	0.15
Canada	1.80	1.92	0.12
Germany	2.40	2.78	0.38
Japan	3.02	3.33	0.31
South Korea	2.17	3.36[a]	1.19

Source: GAO analysis of OECD data.

[a]Data for 2008.

The South Korean government has invested in various research institutes, including those that are state-financed, university-based, and private-sector driven. According to Commerce officials in South Korea, every government ministry invests in several research institutes. For example, the Ministry of Science, ICT, and Future Planning supports approximately 25 research institutes, including the Electronics and Telecommunications Research Institute (ETRI), according to ETRI officials. ETRI is a global information technology research institute and the largest government-funded research institute in South Korea—whose work is partly responsible for putting South Korea on the map as a leader in information and communications technology, such as smart phones and mobile computing.

As part of South Korea's 2009 growth strategy, the national government has emphasized its plans to train SMEs, promote R&D, and expand

---

[22] Data for South Korea and the United States are as of 2008 because that is the most current data available for these countries.

green energy technology development. For example, the government provides testing and standardization equipment and labs that SMEs would not otherwise be able to access through various research institutes, according to officials from the Ministry of Trade, Industry, and Energy (formerly known as the Ministry of Knowledge Economy)—the main ministry for manufacturing policy. South Korea also plans to encourage innovation and help make South Korea a world leader in green technology by turning green energy industries—such as renewables and smart grids—into export industries, and encouraging current industries to become green according to government documents.[23]According to national government officials responsible for coordinating South Korea's green growth policies, most green growth programs fit within South Korea's larger manufacturing strategy, and the policy mechanisms that have been used have been integrated into or build on existing programs. These officials stated that existing tax subsidies for emerging industries, including information technology and biotechnology, have recently been extended to green areas. They pointed out that the government provides a R&D tax credit for private firms using green technology: 20 percent of total investment on green technology for large companies, and 30 percent for SMEs.

South Korea has also emphasized the development of a network of technoparks—regional innovation centers that provide manufacturing assets, R&D facilities, business incubation, and education and production assistance to industry—to encourage growth and development throughout the country.[24] For example, Daejeon Technopark (Daejeon) assists with R&D by encouraging collaboration between industry, academia, research institutes, and local government, according to Daejeon officials. Specifically, it connects SMEs to researchers or universities working on related research. It also supports technology

---

[23] South Korea's National Strategy for Green Growth has three main objectives and ten policy directions, based on a consensus between public, private, and academic stakeholders. The three objectives are (1) mitigation of climate change and the strengthening of the country's energy independence; (2) creation of new growth engines; and (3) improvement in quality of life and enhancement of Korea's international standing. Policies include reducing the use of fossil fuels, developing green technology, and becoming a role model for the international community as a green growth leader.

[24] This initiative is, in part, intended to help fuel development outside of Seoul, where most economic activity is centered.

sharing by providing SMEs access to technology, along with the support and expertise of the park's professional staff.

Table 5 highlights examples of manufacturing-related programs in South Korea. For further information on South Korean programs included in this review, see Appendix III.

Table 5: South Korean Programs That Support Manufacturing

Program/ initiative	Program/ initiative description	Budget (in USD millions, fiscal year 2012)	Year founded/ introduced
Innovation			
Daedeok Innopolis	An innovation ecosystem/ cluster that consists of universities, research institutes, government and government-invested institutions, corporate research institutes and venture corporations in several areas, including aerospace, robotics, nuclear and hydro power, and information technology, among others.	No information available	1973
Daejeon Technopark	A government-sponsored technopark that focuses on growing existing enterprises supporting R&D in the information technology, nanotechnology, robotics, and mechatronics industries.[a]	No information available	2002
Electronics and Telecommunications Research Institute	A global information technology research institute and the largest government funded research institute in South Korea, which focuses on mobile technology, among other things.	526	1976
Trade			
Korea Trade-Investment Promotion Agency	The national implementing agency for South Korea's trade and investment goals and policies set by the Ministry of Trade, Industry, and Energy.	No information available	1962

Source: GAO analysis of Daedeok Innopolis; Daejeon Technopark; Electronics and Telecommunications Research Institute; Korea Trade-Investment Promotion Agency documents.

Note: Amounts converted to U.S. dollars from South Korean won and rounded to the nearest million.

[a]Mechatronics is the cross-disciplinary study of mechanical and electrical engineering and computer science.

Foreign Manufacturing Programs Offer Some Key Contrasts to Those in the United States

When compared to the United States, the countries in our study offer some key distinctions in government programs to support the manufacturing sector.[25] Based on our comparison of selected U.S. programs, the foreign countries place a stronger emphasis on innovation programs that support commercialization, especially through programs that provide technical support and product development and support for infrastructure and clusters. In contrast, the United States spends a relatively high amount on competitive funding for R&D projects with commercial potential. Within trade policy, countries in our study all provide similar services but there are several differences in how they are delivered. For example, the United States is an acknowledged leader in intellectual property protection, but the United States government plays a less prominent role than Japan in developing technological standards. Regarding training programs, Germany's national government has a long history of managing a dual training system to provide graduates with vocational training and nationally recognized credentials and help ensure a supply of skilled manufacturing workers. The United States does not have a comparable program on such a scale. However, some federal, local, and private sector entities in the United States are taking steps to provide work-based and academic learning tailored to manufacturers' needs and develop a framework for nationally portable credentials. In assessing differences among countries in program funding levels, it is important to keep in mind that higher relative funding levels may not necessarily produce better outcomes.

Commercialization Is a Key Goal of Foreign Innovation Programs

While the United States and the four countries we studied all provide support for innovation and R&D, Canada, Germany, Japan, and South Korea have made commercialization a central goal of their innovation programs. Each of the four foreign countries has taken a multi-pronged approach to spur innovation and help manufacturers bridge the "valley of death" between concept and market. The programs they implement to achieve these goals place a particular emphasis on bringing SMEs into the innovation process. Innovation programs abroad incorporate three broad strategies: (1) providing technical support and product development for client firms, especially SMEs; (2) fostering collaboration between manufacturers and researchers, as well as between small and large

---

[25] The findings in this section cite various U.S. programs as examples to illustrate broad points of comparison between policies in our four study countries and the United States. We did not perform a comprehensive review of U.S. programs that support manufacturing.

manufacturers; and (3) providing competitive grants for private-sector R&D efforts with commercial potential. While the United States offers many similar types of programs, the programs we identified offer somewhat less extensive support for technical support and product development than those in some foreign countries, but relatively high funding for R&D grants.[26]

Technical Support and Product Development

Canada, Germany, and Japan have set up national networks of centers that provide a wide range of hands-on technical and business support services to manufacturing firms, especially SMEs. The focus of many of these programs suggests that they see SMEs as a rich potential source of innovation that market barriers, such as the financial risks of conducting R&D, might impede without government support. For example, Japan's Tokyo Metropolitan Industrial Research Institute (TIRI), one center among the national Kohsetsushi network of 182 centers, offers a wide array of services and facilities to SMEs, including testing services, laboratories for product development, information on international technical standards, and intellectual property support. TIRI also offers collaborative research partners for SMEs to engage in R&D for product and technology development. Germany's Fraunhofer Institutes also operate an extensive network of nationwide centers—serving both SMEs and large manufacturers—that offer university-affiliated research expertise to clients. According to Fraunhofer officials, product and technology commercialization are central objectives of their centers. Canada's Industrial Research Assistance Program (IRAP), that country's national SME support network, emphasizes the role of expert technical advisers in helping clients commercialize their products through expertise with R&D, networking, and business strategy.

The United States has a comparable program in the Hollings Manufacturing Extension Partnership (MEP) network of technical support centers aimed at SMEs, which is administered by Commerce's NIST. MEP operates a national network of 60 centers to provide support to SME manufacturers, focusing on helping manufacturers in five key areas: (1) technology acceleration, (2) supplier development, (3) sustainability, (4)

---

[26] Various studies have examined government policies to support innovation and manufacturing. For example, see McKinsey Global Institute and McKinsey Operations Practice, *Manufacturing the Future: The Next Era of Global Growth and Innovation* (Nov. 2012) and National Research Council of the National Academies, *Rising to the Challenge: U.S. Innovation Policy for the Global Economy* (Washington, D.C.: 2012).

workforce, and (5) continuous improvement. Specifically, MEP centers enter into contracts with companies to deliver technical assistance to improve their manufacturing processes and productivity, expand capacity, adopt new technologies, utilize best management practices, and accelerate company growth. However, MEP officials with whom we spoke said that MEP centers offer a more limited focus on commercialization, and do not typically offer testing equipment or widespread expertise in product commercialization. Instead, MEP may connect client firms to third parties offering specific services.

As table 6 shows, Canada, Germany, and Japan invest more money and resources in their technical support programs than the United States does in MEP. According to NIST officials, MEP receives about $100 million in government funding, and two-thirds of its revenues comes from other sources such as client fees, states, or other partner resources. Canada's IRAP, in comparison, had funding of $143 million (U.S.) in 2011-12, with an expanded budget of $257.6 million for 2012-13, a much higher investment relative to the size of the economy or the manufacturing sector than the United States. Further, according to IRAP officials, it provides its client services for free. MEP's technical staff number approximately 1,300, a much larger number than IRAP, but Japan's and Germany's programs exceed the MEP in funding and the number of technical staff.

Table 6: Comparison of National Technical Support and Product Development Programs

Country (example program)	Government funding, 2012 (in USD millions)	Number of centers	Number of technical staff	Charges client fees
United States (MEP)	$100	60	1,300	Yes
Canada (IRAP)	$258	Over 100	Over 200	No
Germany (Fraunhofer)	$595	60	15,000	Yes
Japan (Kohsetsushi)	$2,140	182	6,000	Yes[a]

Source: GAO analysis of program information.

[a]TIRI, one Kohsetsushi site, charges client fees, according to TIRI officials. We could not confirm if this holds true for all Kohsetsushi centers in Japan.

Fostering Collaboration through Infrastructure and Cluster Support

Innovation vouchers

- Innovation vouchers—credits that SMEs can use to purchase services from public knowledge providers—have gained attention as a strategy for spurring innovation. According to an ITIF official, they have been introduced in Austria, Belgium, Canada, Denmark, Germany, Ireland, the Netherlands, and Sweden.

- Proponents say that innovation vouchers offer a simple approach to increasing both SME access to research-intensive technology and disseminating SME-created technologies.

- Vouchers usually range in value from $5,000 to $30,000, according to the ITIF official.

- In the United States, Connecticut has launched an innovation voucher program in which businesses can apply for vouchers worth up to $10,000, which the firm can use to pay a service provider to complete clearly defined business or technology development projects, according to state documents.

Canada, Germany, Japan, and South Korea also encourage manufacturing commercialization through programs that facilitate collaboration between manufacturers and researchers. Specifically, several foreign programs we analyzed support collaboration by providing access to facilities and funding for business clusters—almost a literal implementation of investment in the industrial "commons" —with programs that have been in operation longer than those in the United States. Japan's Kawasaki-region business incubation centers provide office space, research laboratories and testing facilities. South Korea's Daedeok Innopolis consists of universities, research institutes, government and government-invested institutions, corporate research institutes and venture corporations. These programs may encourage opportunities for applied R&D and product development not only through access to facilities, but also through interaction among companies in close physical proximity to each other. According to program officials, Japan's TAMA Association, one site among 18 in the country's Industrial Cluster project, and South Korea's Daedeok Innopolis help SMEs match technologies they develop with larger companies that may be able to apply these technologies to products they make, or processes for making them, which may increase technology dissemination. Germany's Spitzencluster program has encouraged cluster formation by providing funding to clusters judged to be among the country's best, or "leading edge"; the program has awarded three rounds of funding of up to approximately $257 million per round to 15 total selected clusters. Canada offers manufacturers access to research facilities to conduct R&D in various scientific fields through its National Research Council.

In the United States, the federal government has recently begun to increase support for clusters. The Small Business Administration (SBA) Regional Innovation Cluster Initiative, a U.S. federal government cluster program piloted in 2010, has funded 10 existing U.S. clusters, with 7 clusters receiving funding of $2.7 million in FY 2012, according to SBA. SBA's 1-year evaluation of the initiative showed positive results, including over two-thirds of participating businesses reporting development of a new product, and over half commercializing new technology. In 2011, several federal partners, led by the Economic Development Administration, funded the Jobs and Innovation Accelerator Challenge (JIAC), the first interagency cluster initiative. JIAC provided $37 million to 20 existing clusters. Later in 2011, $9 million was awarded to 13 clusters in rural areas. In 2012, the 3rd JIAC awarded $20.2 million to 10 existing clusters focusing on Advanced Manufacturing.

Table 7 provides a comparison of spending across countries on cluster support programs.

Table 7: Comparison of Cluster Programs

Country (program)	Government funding, 2012 (in USD millions)	Number of sites	Year established
United States (SBA Regional Innovation Cluster Initiative)	2.7	7	2010
United States (Jobs and Innovation Accelerator Challenge--JIAC)	37[a]	20	2011
United States (Rural JIAC)	9[a]	13	2011
United States (Advanced Manufacturing JIAC)	20.2	10	2012
Japan (Industrial Clusters Project)	177.4[b]	18	2001
S. Korea (Daedeok Innopolis)	45.8	100	1973
Germany (Spitzencluster)	77[c]	15	2007

Source: GAO analysis of program information.

[a]Figure for 2011

[b]Figure for 2009.

[c]The Spitzencluster program awards 5 clusters a total of $51M each for a 5-year period. Over the 2007-2017 period, a total of approximately $771 million in national government funding will be spent on Spitzencluster; this figure represents the annual average of that funding.

Competitive Funding for R&D Projects with Commercial Potential

Another way countries support commercialization is through competitive funding programs that evaluate and fund private manufacturing R&D projects with commercial potential. Japan's New Energy and Industrial Technology Development Organization (NEDO) was established in 1980 to promote the development of new energy technologies but has since broadened its scope to fund industrial R&D projects. NEDO officials said that a typical project they fund would have a budget of $12.5 million for five years. NEDO's overall budget for 2012 was approximately $1.6 billion. Germany funds R&D through the Central Innovation Program for SMEs, which focuses on SMEs and business-related research establishments cooperating with them. The program funds up to half of a business's costs for technical support, technology transfer, training, and other activities in the development of a new product or process, and has government funding of about $643 million per year. The Canadian Innovation Commercialization Program (CICP), with funding of approximately $32 million (U.S.) per year, is a federal program that helps companies bridge the pre-commercialization gap for their innovative goods and services, in part by testing innovative goods and services within the Canadian government before taking them to the marketplace.

The United States devotes a large amount of money to competitively-awarded R&D funding relative to other countries we studied. SBA administers two large funding programs through the Small Business Innovation Research (SBIR) and Small Business Technology Transfer (STTR) programs. The funds for the SBIR program are provided by federal agencies with an extramural budget of at least $100 million for research or R&D, and for STTR by agencies with extramural research or R&D budgets of at least $1 billion; SBA oversees the programs and the efforts of these agencies. According to SBA officials, the SBIR and STTR programs had combined budgets of approximately $2.5 billion in 2012 to fund awards in successive phases, designed to promote technological innovation and economic growth within small businesses. Generally, the agencies participating in the SBIR and STTR programs offer up to $150,000 to awardees for an initial 6-month period of performance, and those applicants who receive a subsequent phase award typically receive up to $1 million for a 2–year period of performance. SBA officials said that projects are often evaluated for potential commercial applications to the evaluating agency itself, such as the Department of Defense, as opposed to potential demand for the product from the private sector (although this varies by agency). This aspect of SBIR/STTR takes a similar approach to Canada's CICP in that it uses government procurement as a means for potentially introducing innovative products into the larger market. Table 8 compares funding for some countries' R&D grant programs.

Table 8: Comparison of Funding for R&D Grant Programs

Country (program)	Government funding, 2012 (in USD millions)
United States (SBIR/STTR)	2,500
Canada (CICP)	32[a]
Japan (NEDO)	1,600
Germany (ZIM)	643

Source: GAO analysis of program information.

[a]Canadian officials reported that the CICP received a total of $95 million over a 3–year period beginning in 2010.

Countries Continue to See Trade as an Important Component of Manufacturing Policy

In each of the countries we studied, trade policy is an important part of manufacturing policy, and each country's approach shares commonalities with the others. Every country we studied—including the United States—focuses on export promotion, harmonization of standards, and protection of intellectual property rights.[27] Canadian, German, Japanese, South Korean, and U.S. export promotion programs offer help in market identification and development. However, there are some differences. For example, in Japan, efforts to promote and harmonize product standards are supported by the government in conjunction with industrial leaders, but in the United States, they are led by the private sector in most cases. All five countries also provide information to help businesses establish or protect intellectual property rights as a way to encourage innovation and help ensure that manufactured goods can be sold abroad.

Export Promotion

According to the World Trade Organization, in 2011, Canada, Germany, Japan, South Korea, and the United States were among the world's largest exporters of manufactured goods—accounting for about $3.7 trillion in manufactured exports (or about 32 percent of the global export value in this category).[28] These countries generally offer similar types of export promotion services to domestic businesses, including assistance for participation in trade fairs, participation in trade missions, data and market analytics, and services targeted towards SMEs. However, there are some differences in how they provide these services. For example:

- According to Canada's Trade Commissioner Service officials, the Trade Commissioner Service manages the Export USA program, which helps Canadian SMEs understand the specific legal fundamentals of exporting to the United States, Canada's largest trading partner.
- According to State and Commercial Service officials at the U.S. embassy in Berlin, Germany's trade fair system is key to German manufacturers' success because it helps create awareness of global trends in different sectors, and showcases Germany as a place to do business.

---

[27] We did not conduct a comprehensive survey of trade policy tools in these three areas that countries in our study use to support manufacturing.

[28] *International Trade and Tariff Data*, in the World Trade Organization's International Trade and Market Access Data online (includes the 'manufactures' sector in the 'exports' trade flow category), accessed June 19, 2013, http://www.wto.org.

- According to TIRI officials, Japan's Metropolitan Technical Support Network for Export Products—a cooperative initiative of nine prefecture-based research institutes—offers consultation and information on international product standards to SMEs for export products, as well as testing to determine compliance with those standards.
- According to officials from South Korea's Korea Trade-Investment Promotion Agency, 99 Korea Business Centers around the world can be used as SME branch offices. The Korea Trade-Investment Promotion Agency also manages logistics centers—operated with UPS or DHL—to facilitate Korean firms' distribution operations overseas.

Canada, Germany, Japan, South Korea, and the United States also differ in the amount of resources they provide for export promotion and the number of locations that their export promotion efforts reach. For example, according to a recent U.S. International Trade Administration study, while all of these countries employ expert staff abroad to assist with the exporting process, the total number of staff varies somewhat, with the United States and Japan employing the fewest export promotion personnel (see table 9).[29]

Table 9: Number of Export Promotion Personnel and Number of Countries where Export Promotion Activities Are Conducted by Five Countries

Country[a]	Number of export promotion personnel	Number of countries where export promotion activities are conducted
Canada	2,308	99
Germany	2,227	85
Japan	1,545	57
South Korea	1,650	72
United States	1,545	72[b]

Source: International Trade Administration data, Commercial Service data, and foreign trade agency websites.

[a]Canada amounts as of 2011-2012; Germany as of 2012; Japan as of 2011; South Korea as of 2010; United States as of 2012.

[29] The scope of this study is limited to foreign competitor government programs that are the equivalent to the International Trade Administration's export promotion mandate, including the work of the International Trade Administration's U.S. and Foreign Commercial Service, Market Access and Compliance, and Manufacturing and Services units. Many other U.S. agencies provide export promotion services, which are not included in this study. See also GAO, *Export Promotion: Better Information Needed about Federal Resources,* GAO-13-644 (Washington, D.C.: July 17, 2013).

Similarly, although the amount of export promotion funding does not vary greatly across the countries in our study—from $226 to $381 million—the United States spends less on export promotion per $1000 of GDP and per $1000 of exports than many other similarly-situated countries, including Canada, Japan, and South Korea (see Table 10).

Table 10: Export Promotion Budgets of Five Countries Relative to GDP and Export Volume[a]

	Export promotion budget[b] (in USD millions)	GDP[c] (in USD billions)	Export promotion budget per $1000 GDP	Exports[d] (in USD billions)	Export promotion budget per $1000 of exports
Canada	296	1,759	$0.17	455	$0.65
Germany	226	3,629	$0.06	1,501	$0.15
Japan	285	5,855	$0.05	909	$0.31
South Korea	289	1,164	$0.25	548	$0.53
United States	381	15,094	$0.03	1,796	$0.21

Source: International Trade Administration data.

[a]According to the International Trade Administration, there are limitations to quantitative comparisons of direct foreign counterparts on the export promotion programs being analyzed. The government and commercial fabric in some foreign competitor countries is sufficiently different from that of the United States that direct comparisons of government expenditures are difficult. For example, in Germany, Japan, and Korea, government and industry collaborate, which means that government expenditures on export promotion shown here understate the total expenditures on export promotion. Further, all countries in this analysis provide subsidies to businesses in some form.

[b]Canada amounts as of 2011-2012; Germany as of 2012; Japan as of 2011; South Korea as of 2010; United States as of 2012.

[c]As of 2011.

[d]As of 2010.

Further, the four other countries in our review have a single agency primarily responsible for implementing export promotion, whereas the United States has several. For example, in the United States, the Trade Promotion Coordinating Committee (TPCC), an interagency task force, includes 20 agencies that participate in export promotion. Of the 20 TPCC agencies, seven are considered core agencies.[30] In contrast, Canada's

---

[30] TPCC core agencies are Commerce, Export-Import Bank, Overseas Private Investment Corporation, U.S. Trade and Development Agency, Small Business Administration, State, and Department of Agriculture. The TPCC is chaired by the Secretary of Commerce and the Under Secretary of Commerce for International Trade.

GAO-13-365 Global Manufacturing

Trade Commissioner Service, Germany's Association of Chambers of Commerce and Industry, and South Korea's Korea Trade-Investment Promotion Agency implement export promotion programs in their respective countries. We previously reported that Commerce's Foreign Commercial Service activities align with relevant National Export Initiative trade promotion priorities, but that in an environment of limited resources, systematic use of economic, performance and activity data could help allocate resources to achieve its goals more efficiently and effectively.[31]

International Standards

Although the United States and Japan both view international standards as an important component of manufacturing policy, they have different mechanisms for setting voluntary standards on industrial products. In the United States, the government primarily coordinates standards on industrial products through the private sector, whereas Japan's national government plays a more active role in setting and enforcing standards.[32]

According to documents from the Japanese Industrial Standards Committee (JISC), a committee of up to 30 knowledgeable experts comprised of members from the national government, private sector, industry associations, and academia, METI administers the national standards system by drafting and enforcing standards-related laws and regulations. According to the committee, four additional government ministries have the ability to set standards with input from the committee. Japan's Next Generation Vehicle program illustrates the government's active role in trying to influence international technical standards for manufacturing. According to NIST officials, the South Korean government also plays an active role in trying to influence international technical standards for manufacturing through standards as well as conformity assessment requirements.

In the United States, NIST acts as a coordinator in getting manufacturers to adopt standards and provides services to assist manufacturers in implementing manufacturing standards but has no regulatory power to

---

[31] GAO: *National Export Initiative: U.S. and Foreign Commercial Service Should Improve Performance and Resource Allocation Management*, GAO-11-909 (Washington, D.C.: Sep. 29, 2011); *Export Promotion: Increases in Commercial Service Workforce Should be Better Planned*, GAO-10-874 Washington, D.C. (August 31, 2010). See also Executive Order No. 13534.

[32] We did not review mechanisms for setting standards on industrial products in Canada or Germany because these countries' practices did not meet our selection criteria.

enforce them, according to NIST and industry officials. According to NIST officials, hundreds of private sector organizations, including professional societies, trade associations, testing and certifying organizations, and industry consortia develop standards through an open, consensus-based process. Among other things, NIST coordinates the use of private sector standards by federal agencies, states, and local governments to avoid the development of duplicative standards. In addition, NIST scientists and engineers work with the private sector to develop standards that are based on sound science and ensure that the standards are supported by effective measurements, test methods, and appropriate conformity assessment systems.

Intellectual Property Rights

We did not identify any key differences between the four foreign countries and the United States with regard to protecting intellectual property rights. All of the foreign countries we studied promote R&D to create intellectual property and support manufacturers by protecting intellectual property rights through various mechanisms. See appendix III for details on how various programs support intellectual property rights. The United States is an acknowledged global leader in the creation of intellectual property, and has generally advocated strong intellectual property protection.

Germany's Sustained Commitment to Vocational Training Helps Provide a Supply of Skilled Manufacturing Workers

Germany's national government has maintained a substantial commitment to a dual training system, which helps provide a supply of skilled workers for the manufacturing sector. In particular, Germany's system has a long history of building public-private partnerships to develop curriculum and standards and providing graduates with nationally-recognized, portable credentials. While not on the same scale as the German dual training system, some federal and local entities in the United States are taking steps to provide a combination of work-based and academic learning to meet manufacturers' needs through public-private partnerships. In addition, Labor, some U.S. states, and Canada's federal government have taken steps to encourage participation in their apprenticeship programs to train workers in the skilled trades needed by manufacturers. While the United States does not have a national system to issue industry-recognized credentials, the manufacturing industry, with participation from the federal government, has recently started moving in this direction.

Germany's dual training system facilitates broad consensus among stakeholders in business, labor, and education, which in turn creates a supply of workers with skills needed in the manufacturing sector. The national government enforces the dual training system's regulations and has coordinated with industry, union, and state government stakeholders to develop skill standards in 350 occupations. One agency, the Federal Institute for Vocational Education and Training, is responsible for conducting education and labor market research, facilitating regular stakeholder coordination among public agencies and private industry associations on needed skills, and managing changes to the system's standards. The Federal Institute for Vocational Education and Training was established in 1970 and, given its central role in bringing stakeholders together, its board is referred to as the "parliament" of vocational education. Some experts note that this unified approach and cooperative relationship among the various stakeholders are strengths of this system, and representatives of German government and industry cited the system as an important support to the manufacturing sector. Moreover, Germany has a high overall societal acceptance of the need for the dual training system. In addition, support for training and for the skilled trades is deeply embedded in German society, and about 55 percent of high school students enter the dual training system each year.

In contrast, the United States and Canada have a more decentralized system of skills training programs, with management of these programs largely devolved to states and localities. In the United States, Labor has a major role in administering a number of federally-funded skills training programs, including those under the Workforce Investment Act of 1998 (WIA), which largely target dislocated workers and economically disadvantaged adults and youth.[33] WIA programs are overseen at the local level by Workforce Investment Boards, committees of local business, labor, and government representatives, with services provided through local American Job Centers.[34] Labor also administers a Registered Apprenticeship Program, which offers assistance in creating on-the-job training programs in accordance with accepted skills certification organizations in relevant disciplines. Registered apprenticeship programs are sponsored on a voluntary basis by individual

---

[33] Labor's Trade Adjustment Assistance program funds employment and training services to manufacturing workers who lose their jobs as a result of international trade.

[34] WIA created a comprehensive workforce investment system that brought together multiple federally funded employment and training programs into a single system called the One-Stop system. The One-Stop system is composed of One-Stop Career Centers around the country that are designed to provide a full range of assistance to job seekers, including training referrals, career counseling, and job listings. In 2012, Labor changed the name of One-Stop Career Centers to American Job Centers.

employers, employer associations, or labor-employer agreements, and are federally administered by Labor in 25 states and by state apprenticeship agencies in 25 states. In addition, the Department of Education plays a major role in supporting career and technical education in community colleges and regional and technical centers through the Carl D. Perkins Career and Technical Education Improvement Act of 2006 (Perkins Act).

Unlike Germany, U.S. officials and experts reported that the United States does not have widespread societal support for vocational education and training for the skilled trades, although some federal and local entities are taking steps to target training to meet manufacturers' needs through public-private partnerships. For example, at the federal level, Labor and the Department of Education are providing $2 billion over 4 years to community colleges around the country through the Trade Adjustment Assistance Community College and Career Training initiative. The grants support partnerships between community colleges and employers to develop instructional programs for workers dislocated by international competition that meet specific industry needs, including the manufacturing industry. At the local level, community and technical colleges provide skills training under WIA and the Perkins Act, and in many areas, work closely with employers to develop customized training in key disciplines where workers are needed. One example of this customized training is a partnership that the German corporation Siemens has established with Central Piedmont Community College in North Carolina in order to create a pipeline of skilled workers for manufacturing plants located in the area. Participating students work at Siemens while taking courses in the college's mechatronics degree program.[35] Siemens pays each student's tuition costs, while the participant earns a paycheck and receives company-specific technical training and hands-on experience. Our recent report highlighted similar efforts of Workforce Investment Boards in various locations, including California, Colorado, Illinois, Kansas and Michigan to build public-private partnerships and tailor training programs to meet the specific needs of manufacturers.[36] In addition, some states in the United States have taken steps to focus on

---

[35] Mechatronics is the cross-disciplinary study of mechanical and electrical engineering.

[36] See GAO, *Workforce Investment Act: Innovative Collaborations between Workforce Boards and Employers Helped Meet Local Needs*, GAO-12-97 (Washington, D.C.: January 19, 2012).

skilled trades needed by manufacturers. For example, according to state documents, South Carolina's Personal Pathways to Success system combines academic training with options for work-based learning in 16 career clusters, including manufacturing.

In Canada, apprenticeship programs are primarily administered by the 13 provincial or territorial governments. According to Canadian officials, in recognition of the economic need for apprentices and to increase participation in provincial and territorial apprenticeship programs, the Canadian government offers incentives for continuing and completing an apprenticeship within the country's Red Seal program, which encompasses 55 trades and includes skills needed in the manufacturing sector. In addition, these officials noted that the Canadian government also offers a tax credit for businesses that hire apprentices and a tax deduction for the purchase of tools by any eligible apprentice.[37] See Appendix III for more information on Canada's programs.

Unlike Germany and Canada, the United States has no unified national system through which credentials are granted or skills are assessed, though the manufacturing industry, with participation from the federal government, has recently started moving in this direction. Germany's dual training system provides graduates with a nationally recognized credential upon finishing a program of study. Similarly, Canada's Red Seal program offers an exam for apprentices to take at the end of their training to obtain a nationally recognized certification of advanced skill. In this way, the German dual training system and the Red Seal exam establish nationally recognized standards of competency, which German officials told us has played a role in facilitating labor mobility, and Canadian officials told us this has played a role in facilitating national recognition of trade qualifications. In contrast, the United States currently has many different types of organizations that award various credentials.[38] However, the Manufacturing Institute, with participation from Labor, Commerce, and other entities, recently launched the Skills Certification System, which

---

[37] In addition, according to Labor, South Carolina has increased the number of Registered Apprenticeship programs in the state by offering a tax incentive of $1,000 per apprentice employed for at least seven months during each year of an apprentice's program, for up to four years of such a program.

[38] Labor defines a credential as a recognition of an individual's attainment of measurable technical or occupational skills necessary to obtain employment or advance within an occupation.

aims to provide a unified framework to align skills certifications from various industry associations with Labor's Advanced Manufacturing Competency Model.[39] According to the Manufacturing Institute, the Skills Certification System is intended to establish a comprehensive set of nationally portable, industry-recognized credentials to validate the skills and competencies needed to be productive in any manufacturing environment. Currently, the Skills Certification System endorses industry certifications in several areas, including machining and metalworking; automation; fabrication; mechatronics; and transportation, distribution, and logistics. While federal and private sector entities are collaborating on this effort, the more established German system suggests that it will require a long-term, sustained commitment and coordination between federal and state authorities to bring such an effort to fruition on a large scale.

Concluding Observations

As the United States considers policies to enhance the global competitiveness of its manufacturing sector, the actions other economically-advanced countries have taken to improve their competitive edge in manufacturing are of particular interest. The manufacturing policies and programs in each of the four countries we examined are shaped by each country's unique political, social, cultural, and economic characteristics and may not be readily applicable to the United States. However, their manufacturing approaches suggest some key areas that the United States may wish to consider as it continues to formulate its manufacturing strategy and programs to carry out that strategy. Each of the foreign countries took a multi-faceted and hands-on approach to spur innovation in ways that are intended to lead to commercialization, suggesting that no one program or mechanism can fully address the challenge of bridging the gap between innovative ideas and manufacturing sales. In addition, we noted the sustained government commitment to managing a national system of vocational skills training and credentialing that facilitates consensus among business, labor, and education. This was particularly evident in Germany. The United States

---

[39] The Manufacturing Institute is a non-profit research organization affiliated with the National Association of Manufacturers. The National Association of Manufacturers is a trade association that encourages the expansion of manufacturing in the United States. Labor, in partnership with manufacturing industry groups, created the Advanced Manufacturing Competency Model as a roadmap of the skills needed by workers in various trades in the manufacturing sector.

has no corollary, and due to major cultural differences it is unlikely that we would consider a similar system of the same scale. However, some recent examples of public-private partnerships established to target training for the manufacturing sector and develop a set of nationally portable, industry-recognized credentials show how certain aspects of the German dual training system might be applied through incremental actions.

More generally, our analysis of the manufacturing programs in the four selected countries shows the broad extent to which U.S. competitors are leveraging the public sector to help their manufacturing industries maintain competitiveness in a rapidly changing global economy. Their programs involve a partnership of government and the private sector, with varying but shared responsibilities for supporting applied R&D and commercialization efforts; facilities for research, testing and production; and expertise and services. Many of these programs go beyond a more traditional government role of setting incentives, establishing regulations, and providing funding. In the end, the best guide to devising U.S. manufacturing policy may be to think about how the mix of existing and proposed federal programs fits into our unique economic context and can provide the most benefit to the economy at large.

Agency and Third-Party Comments and Our Evaluation

We sent a draft of this report to Commerce, Labor, and State, and selected draft report sections to SBA, the Department of Education, and the Department of Energy. Commerce, Labor, SBA, and Energy provided technical comments, which we incorporated, as appropriate. State and Education did not have comments. We also sent draft report sections to foreign officials to verify information on foreign programs that support manufacturing, and incorporated technical comments from these officials, as appropriate.

As agreed with your office, unless you publicly announce its contents earlier, we plan no further distribution until 30 days after the date of this letter. At that time, we will send copies to the Secretaries of Commerce, Labor, and State, appropriate congressional committees, and other interested parties. In addition, the report is available at no charge on the GAO website at http://www.gao.gov.

If you or your staff have any questions about this report, please contact Andrew Sherrill at (202) 512-7215 or SherrillA@gao.gov; or Lawrance Evans at (202) 512-4802 or EvansL@gao.gov. Contact points for our

Offices of Congressional Relations and Public Affairs may be found on the last page of this report. GAO staff who made key contributions to this report are listed in appendix IV.

Sincerely Yours,

Andrew Sherrill
Director, Education, Workforce,
  and Income Security Issues

Lawrance L. Evans, Jr.
Director, International Affairs and Trade

Appendix I: Objectives, Scope, and Methodology

Our key objectives for this report ask:

1. What government strategies and programs have other advanced economies implemented to approach issues similar to those facing manufacturing in the United States?

2. What key distinctions exist between policy approaches to support manufacturing in other advanced economies and those in the United States?

We selected four study countries—Canada, Germany, Japan, and South Korea— and the programs that support manufacturing in each country based on several factors. Since we focused on "similarly situated" countries for comparison to the United States, we considered primarily high-GDP countries that have democratic governments. We contacted approximately 20 experts whose career involved studying or advocating for manufacturing policy; these included representatives from industry associations, labor, academia, think tanks, and trade groups.[1] We interviewed these experts about key manufacturing issues and obtained their views about which foreign countries had innovative programs to support manufacturing. We also asked officials from the Departments of Labor (Labor) and Commerce (Commerce) to comment on some of the selected foreign programs recommended by experts. We conducted additional research on the programs in the countries experts mentioned. To make our final country selection, we considered factors such as the number of experts that mentioned a country as a candidate for study and the number and breadth of programs our research indicated each country offered.

We then worked with officials from the U.S Department of State (State) stationed in our selected countries and foreign embassy officials to finalize programs for our review, based on our research and the recommendations of the foreign officials. We did not attempt to perform a comprehensive review of programs that support manufacturing in the four selected foreign countries, nor did we seek information in all countries about programs in each of our three key policy categories—innovation, trade, and training. For example, in some countries, we did not examine training or trade programs because through expert opinion, input from

---

[1] We identified experts primarily through a "snowball" approach, in which we contacted people we interviewed for suggestions of other people we should contact.

U.S. officials, and our literature review, we did not identify programs in
these areas as being particularly informative for U.S. policy.

To obtain specific program information, we traveled to each country to
interview foreign officials overseeing each program. We also analyzed
documents with key program information that these officials provided. We
did not analyze or review foreign laws or regulations, and relied on
program information, including budget information, from sources provided
by foreign agency officials and other sources. We also sent report
excerpts to foreign officials to verify information on the programs and
incorporated technical comments from these officials where appropriate.
Moreover, we did not evaluate the effectiveness of any foreign programs.
Because we did not conduct original analyses, none of the program
descriptions regarding foreign programs in this report should be
considered GAO assessments or evaluations of those programs.

To identify key differences in manufacturing policies between our selected
foreign countries and those in the United States, we synthesized our
analyses of the foreign programs we examined to identify common and
unique features among them. We then researched comparable programs
in the United States, in part based on suggestions from Commerce and
Labor, and interviewed staff at agencies administering those programs.
We did not attempt to conduct a comprehensive review of U.S.
manufacturing policy or programs, nor did we evaluate the effectiveness
of U.S. programs.

This report uses data obtained from large U.S. and international agencies
and from foreign manufacturing agencies. We assessed the reliability of
data from the Bureau of Labor Statistics, the Bureau of Economic
Analysis, World Bank, and Organisation for Economic Co-operation and
Development (OECD) by reviewing literature provided by the
organizations regarding their methodology for compiling data, including
measures to ensure data quality and comparability across countries. We
determined that these data were sufficiently reliable for the purposes of
our report. Regarding data provided by foreign agencies, we did not
independently attempt to confirm provided data except where
documentary evidence provided by those agencies allowed us to do so.
However, we did confirm the accuracy of the figures and our use of them

by having foreign officials review relevant excerpts of the report.[2] We found these data to be sufficiently reliable for our purposes.

For data on export promotion, we assessed the reliability of data from the World Trade Organization by reviewing literature provided by that organization regarding its methodology for compiling data, including the use of the international standard system for categorizing exports. We contacted cognizant Commerce officials with respect to an International Trade Administration study that compared and analyzed foreign countries' export promotion budget levels, and with respect to data on the number of countries where the United States conducts export promotion activities. We reviewed the steps Commerce officials took in collecting and analyzing the data, and we found the data to be sufficiently reliable for our purposes.

We obtained data on the number of countries in which Canada, Germany, Japan, and South Korea conduct export promotion activities using their officially released information on their governments' website. We confirmed these numbers with cognizant Canadian, German, and South Korean officials. We were unable to confirm the number of countries in which Japan conducts export promotion activities with cognizant officials. We believe these sources are sufficiently reliable for the purpose of our report.

We conducted this performance audit from March 2012 to July 2013 in accordance with generally accepted government auditing standards. Those standards require that we plan and perform the audit to obtain sufficient, appropriate evidence to provide a reasonable basis for our findings and conclusions based on our audit objectives. We believe that the evidence obtained provides a reasonable basis for our findings and conclusions based on our audit objectives.

---

[2] We converted program budget and other foreign expenditure numbers into U.S. currency by using the average annual exchange rate, as reported by OECD, for the applicable year for the nominal figure. For example, to convert 2012 program expenditures, we used the average exchange rate for 2012.

Appendix II: Examples of Recent U.S. Manufacturing Policy Initiatives

In recent years, both Congress and the Administration have taken steps to help define the goals and broad principles of a U.S. manufacturing strategy.[1] The America COMPETES Reauthorization Act of 2010 aimed in part to increase the nation's R&D investment in science and engineering research and in science, technology, engineering, and mathematics education. This law required the establishment of new programs, including Commerce's Regional Innovation Program; required the establishment of a committee involved in STEM education; and required the establishment of an Advisory Council on Innovation and Entrepreneurship. In addition, it outlines requirements for various government agencies relating to improving the competitiveness of the manufacturing sector in the United States. It also created an interagency Committee on Technology under the National Science & Technology Council responsible for planning and coordinating federal programs and activities in advanced manufacturing. The act also directs Commerce to (1) analyze taxes, regulations, and the economy; trade and export policies; workforce issues; and barriers to U.S. competitiveness; and (2) develop a 10-year innovation and competitiveness strategy. Furthermore, the America COMPETES Reauthorization Act of 2010 authorized funding for research through the National Science Foundation, the National Institute of Standards and Technology (NIST), the Department of Energy, and Commerce.

Likewise, the Administration has proposed a framework for manufacturing and various initiatives to spur manufacturing. In 2009, the Administration put forth "A Framework for Revitalizing American Manufacturing," which lays out policies in seven areas: (1) providing workers with the opportunity to obtain the skills necessary to be highly productive; (2) investing in the creation of new technologies and business practices; (3) developing stable and efficient capital markets for business investment; (4) helping communities and workers transition to a better future; (5) investing in an advanced transportation infrastructure; (6) ensuring market access and a level playing field; and (7) improving the general business climate, especially for manufacturing. The Administration has put forth several other documents laying out its manufacturing strategy since 2009—including "The National Strategic Plan for Advanced Manufacturing," which it published in February 2012 to guide Federal programs and

---

[1] We obtained information on this topic to highlight some examples but did not attempt to develop a comprehensive list of initiatives related to U.S. manufacturing.

activities in support of advanced manufacturing R&D in response to the America COMPETES Reauthorization Act of 2010.[2]

In addition, the Administration has established several manufacturing initiatives.

- First, in 2009, the White House announced the formation of the President's Council of Advisors on Science & Technology (PCAST), an advisory group of the nation's leading scientists and engineers who directly advise the President on matters related to U.S. manufacturing.[3]
- In June 2011, the President launched the Advanced Manufacturing Partnership (AMP), a private-sector-led, national effort that brings together industry, universities, and the federal government to chart a course for investing and developing emerging technologies to create high quality manufacturing jobs and enhance U.S. global competitiveness.[4]
- In December 2011, the Administration established the White House Office of Manufacturing Policy, which has worked with PCAST and AMP to coordinate policy to enable innovation.[5]

In March 2012, the President announced the establishment of the National Network for Manufacturing Innovation (NNMI), one purpose of which is to close the gap between research and development activities and the deployment of technological innovations in domestic production of goods. To accomplish this goal, the NNMI plans to form up to 15

---

[2] See Pub. L. No. 111-358, § 102(b)(7), 124 Stat. 3982, 3986 (2011).

[3] PCAST makes policy recommendations in the many areas where understanding of science, technology, and innovation is essential to strengthening our economy and forming policy that works for the American people.

[4] PCAST recommended a partnership involving government, industry, and academia to identify the most pressing challenges and transformative opportunities to improve technologies, processes and products across the manufacturing sector.

[5] For example, AMP brings together industry, universities, and the federal government to chart a course for investing and furthering the development of the emerging technologies that will create high quality manufacturing jobs and enhance U.S. global competitiveness, PCAST recommended establishing the Advanced Manufacturing National Program Office, which has been done. The Advanced Manufacturing National Program Office includes participation from all federal agencies involved in U.S. manufacturing. Agencies involved are Department of Commerce, Department of Defense, Department of Energy, National Aeronautics and Space Administration, and National Science Foundation.

manufacturing innovation institutes around the country to serve as regional hubs of manufacturing excellence. In August 2012, the National Additive Manufacturing Innovation Institute (NAMII) was formally established in Youngstown, Ohio, as the pilot institute under the NNMI infrastructure. NAMII is a public-private partnership with member organizations from industry, academia, government, and workforce development resources, with a goal to transition additive manufacturing technology to the mainstream U.S. manufacturing sector. Another effort in collaboration with the NAMII is the Department of Energy's Manufacturing Demonstration Facilities, which are collaborative manufacturing communities that share a common R&D infrastructure. The first facility was launched at Oak Ridge National Laboratory in January 2012. This facility will provide equipment, scientists, and engineers to develop new energy-sector technologies for commercial application. In May, 2013, the Administration announced $200 million in funding to open three new manufacturing institutes under the NNMI.

Appendix III: Examples of Government Programs that Support Manufacturing in Canada, Germany, Japan, and South Korea

The following programs illustrate the ways in which Canada, Germany, Japan, and South Korea have pursued manufacturing goals through innovation, training, and trade policies. We did not independently evaluate these programs. Our descriptions are based on interviews with knowledgeable officials and review of relevant program documentation. We analyzed documents with key information that these officials provided, but did not review or analyze the primary source materials for such program information. In addition, we did not analyze or review any foreign laws or regulations. Because we did not conduct original analyses, none of the program descriptions regarding foreign programs in this report should be considered GAO assessments or evaluations of those programs. We also sent report excerpts to foreign officials to verify information on the programs and incorporated technical comments from these officials where appropriate.

Canada

Innovation

Accelerated Capital Cost Allowance

The Accelerated Capital Cost Allowance was first introduced in Canada's 2007 budget. According to Finance Canada officials, the policy allows for a 50 percent depreciation of new investment in machinery and equipment in the manufacturing and processing sector. By allowing a faster tax write-off of eligible investments, this measure may help manufacturers remain competitive in the current global environment. According to Canadian officials, the policy has been extended until 2015. Representatives of the Canadian Manufacturers and Exporters—Canada's major national association of manufacturers—told us that although they have advocated that the policy become permanent, this has not been achieved.

Canadian Innovation Commercialization Program (CICP)

The Canadian Innovation Commercialization Program (CICP) was created to bolster innovation in Canada's business sector and was made permanent in Canada's 2012 budget, with $95 million for 3 years starting in 2013, and $40 million per year thereafter. CICP helps companies bridge the pre-commercialization gap for their innovative goods and services in several ways: (1) awarding contracts to entrepreneurs with pre-commercial innovations, (2) testing and providing feedback to entrepreneurs on the performance of their goods or services, (3) providing innovators with the opportunity to enter the marketplace with new goods and services, and (4) providing information on how to do business with the Government of Canada to enhance procurement opportunities. The Canadian Innovation Commercialization Program targets innovations in the priority areas of environment, safety and security, health, and enabling technologies (e.g., biotechnology).

Scientific Research and Experimental Development (SR&ED) Tax Incentive Program

According to Canadian officials, Canada's Scientific Research and Experimental Development (SR&ED) tax incentive program supports business research and development.

The SR&ED tax incentive program has two components:

1. An income tax deduction, which allows immediate expensing of all eligible expenditures, and;

2. An investment tax credit with the following characteristics:

   - The general rate is 20 percent of qualified expenditures carried out in Canada.
   - An enhanced rate of 35 percent is provided to small and medium-sized Canadian-controlled private corporations on their first $3 million of eligible expenditures.
   - Unused credits earned in a year are generally fully refundable for small and medium-sized Canadian-controlled private corporations on their first $3 million of current expenditures.[1]

Currently, eligible expenditures include most of the costs that are directly related to SR&ED, including salary and wages, materials, and overhead, as well as contracts and capital expenditures (other than most buildings).The 2012 budget announced that, effective January 1, 2014, the general rate would be reduced to 15 percent. In addition, the 2012 budget announced that effective the same date, capital expenses (e.g., equipment and machinery) would be eliminated from eligible SR&ED costs. Finance Canada officials estimated $3.6 billion in SR&ED-associated tax expenditures in 2012.

Industrial Research Assistance Program (IRAP)

Canada's 2012 budget announced the Canadian government's intent to double the funding for the Industrial Research Assistance Program (IRAP). IRAP—a federally-funded nationwide network of over 200 Industrial Technology Advisors with sector-specific expertise who consult with SMEs on conducting research and development—had a budget of

---

[1] Entities other than Canadian-controlled private corporations cannot receive the credit as income, but may use it to offset taxes owed.

$258 million in 2012-2013. IRAP advisors assist SMEs in developing, adopting, and adapting technologies as well as incorporating them into competitive products and leading to potential commercialization. According to IRAP officials, over 80 percent of IRAP clients have 50 or fewer employees. According to the 2012 IRAP survey, 62 percent of participating businesses indicated that the program had enhanced their ability to conduct research and development.

Federal Regional Development Organizations

Canada's five federal regional development organizations are another source of support for innovation. Each agency covers a specific geographic area. The Federal Economic Development Agency for Southern Ontario— the regional development agency that was established most recently— was provided $1 billion in funds to expend from 2009-2014 in support of local economic development and competitiveness. The Federal Economic Development Agency for Southern Ontario has created programs intended to boost private sector investment in start-up companies, help SMEs collaborate with colleges and universities to commercialize new products and services, and develop new technology. For example:

- *Investing in Business Innovation.* The Investing in Business Innovation program boosts private sector investment in start-up businesses and allows for the accelerated development and introduction to market of new products, processes, and practices. It also helps angel investor networks and their associations attract new investment and support the growth of angel investment funds.[2] Eligible recipients include southern Ontario nonprofit angel investor networks, nonprofit organizations that represent angel investor networks, and start-up businesses with fewer than 50 employees who have an investment agreement with recognized angel and/or venture capital investors. Eligible activities include product and process applied research, engineering design, technology development, product testing, marketing studies, certification, proof of concept, piloting and demonstration, problem solving, and commercialization of intellectual property.
- *Technology Development Program.* The Technology Development Program helps research and innovation organizations, the private sector, post-secondary institutions, and nonprofit organizations work

---

[2] Angel investors are high net worth individuals who invest their own money in start-up companies in exchange for part ownership of the business.

together to accelerate the development of technologies that will result in new market opportunities for southern Ontario businesses. Eligible recipients include southern Ontario nonprofit organizations, such as innovation and commercialization organizations, and southern Ontario post-secondary institutions.

- *Applied Research and Commercialization Initiative*. The Applied Research and Commercialization Initiative is designed to address the gap between research and commercialization in southern Ontario by encouraging collaboration between SMEs with pre-market needs and post-secondary institutions with applied research expertise. The goal of the initiative is to accelerate innovation and to improve productivity and competitiveness for businesses located in southern Ontario. Eligible applicants include post-secondary institutions, where SMEs are the primary beneficiary.

Federal Funding for Venture Capital

Canada also sees the lack of venture capital as a challenge to the country's innovation and manufacturing capabilities. To increase the formation and usage of venture capital and encourage innovation, the Canadian government proposed $400 million in venture capital funds in its 2012 budget. The purpose of the venture capital funding is to support early stage risk capital, and to support the creation of large-scale venture capital funds led by the private sector.

Trade

Trade Commissioner Service

Canada's Trade Commissioner Service provides several key export support services to support manufacturers, including:

- *Preparation for international markets*. Trade Commissioner Service offices in Canada help exporting businesses determine whether they are internationally competitive, decide on target markets, collect market and industry information, and help businesses improve their international business strategy.
- *Market intelligence and strategy*. Trade Commissioner Service representatives help businesses determine the level of opportunity that exists in a particular market, appropriate approaches to the market and the amount of effort and resources required by providing up-to-date information on barriers and regulations associated with entering a specific region, as well as information on upcoming opportunities or emerging trends. Trade Commissioner Service provides practical advice in areas such as navigating business and cultural practices, local representation, market entry strategies and participation in global value chains.

- *Provision of qualified contact information.* The Trade Commissioner Service provides exporters with business contacts that include potential buyers and partners, financial and legal professionals, technology sources, manufacturers, foreign regulatory authorities, and foreign investment promotion agencies.
- *Advice to address market access challenges.* The Trade Commissioner Service can advise on market access problems and other business challenges including customs clearance and shipping, unfair business treatment, contract bidding, storage and warehousing, insurance coverage and claims, and overdue accounts receivable.

According to the Trade Commissioner Service, agency staff provided these services to over 14,000 clients from April 2011 to March 2012. Trade Commissioner Service officials told us that many of the clients are manufacturers.

Training

Red Seal Program

Canada also has some programs that provide a framework for skills training related to manufacturing. For example, Canada's Interprovincial Red Seal Program, established in the 1950s, sets national standards for certification of excellence in 55 skilled trades, some of which are within the manufacturing sector. The Red Seal Program provides:

- *National definition of competency.* A national occupational analysis, developed for each Red Seal trade, identifies all the tasks performed in the trade and is used as a base document for the development of interprovincial standard examinations. The provinces and territories are encouraged to use the analysis for curriculum development.
- *Endorsement of advanced skills.* Through the program, apprentices who have completed their training and become certified journeypersons are able to obtain a Red Seal endorsement on their provincial or territorial Certificates of Qualification and Apprenticeship by successfully completing an interprovincial Red Seal examination.

The Red Seal Program is administered by the Canadian Council of Directors of Apprenticeship, a body composed of the Director of Apprenticeship from each province or territory, and representatives of Human Resources and Skills Development Canada, a federal agency. In 2009, the council undertook an evaluation of the Red Seal Program, and determined that increased emphasis on specific, measurable, industry-defined standards and multiple forms of skills assessment would strengthen Canada's apprenticeship system.

| Financial Support for Apprenticeships and Skilled Tradespersons | Canada offers the following financial support to individuals pursuing certification in Red Seal trades: |

- *Apprenticeship grants.* The Apprenticeship Incentive Grant is a taxable grant of $1,000 per year or level, up to a maximum amount of $2,000 per person. It is available to registered apprentices once they have successfully completed their first or second year/level (or equivalent) of an apprenticeship program in one of the Red Seal trades. The Apprenticeship Completion Grant is a taxable grant of $2,000 for registered apprentices who complete their apprenticeship training and obtain their journeyperson certification in a designated Red Seal trade.
- *Cost allowance for tools.* In addition to grants to assist with apprenticeship completion, the Tradesperson's Tools Deduction is a federal tax policy that provides employed tradespersons with an annual deduction of up to $501 to help cover the cost of new tools necessary to their trade. The deduction applies to eligible tools if the total cost exceeds $1,096, and the purchase was made by an employed tradesperson.

Germany

Innovation

| Fraunhofer Institutes | Germany established the Fraunhofer Institutes, a nationwide network of 60 applied research facilities with expert research staff, in 1949 as part of its efforts to rebuild Germany's research infrastructure after World War II, according to Fraunhofer officials. Today, each Fraunhofer institute specializes in a particular subject matter. The 60 institutes are divided into the following categories of specialization: (1) materials and components; (2) microelectronics; (3) information and communications technology; (4) production; (5) light and surfaces, and (6) life sciences. Fraunhofer Institutes are co-located with universities. |

According to Fraunhofer officials, in 2012, the Fraunhofer network had a budget of $2.8 billion. Each individual Fraunhofer Institute's funding is a mix of support from national and state government sources and private sector contracts for research.

- *Applied research collaboration with the private sector on a contractual basis.* Contracts or requests for work from private enterprises are the main way the institutes receive specific research tasks. For each research project, enterprises that have developed a process or technology for potential commercialization enter into a contract for applied research services with the Fraunhofer Institute that has the appropriate subject matter expertise. All Fraunhofer Institutes measure their performance by the number of contracts and the amount of revenue generated by contracts with the private sector.

- *Flexible intellectual property.* In some instances, part of intellectual property can be retained by Fraunhofer, and in some cases, intellectual property can be shared by a combination of Fraunhofer, the university, and the company involved. The technology that was eventually developed into MP3 music files originated in Fraunhofer research, and Fraunhofer currently holds several related patents.

Spitzencluster: Leading Edge Clusters Competition

Germany also supports innovation through various industrial clusters around the country. The Spitzencluster program, the national government's cluster initiative, is intended to strengthen clusters judged through a competitive application process to be the best clusters in the country. Spitzencluster competition winners are selected by an independent jury for demonstrating the ability to pursue strategic objectives in emerging industries identified in Germany's High Tech Strategy 2020. Spitzencluster winners receive up to $51 million over 5 years, and the cluster's participating entities, including businesses and universities, provide the remaining operating costs in a 50-50 cost share arrangement. To date, 15 clusters around the country have received the Spitzencluster designation and are conducting research in a variety of areas, including the following:

- *Information and communication technology.* The Cool Silicon cluster in the region around Dresden develops components and complex system solutions that significantly reduce the energy consumption of information and communications technologies systems. The cluster comprises more than 100 companies and research facilities and is also linked with the Technical Universities of Dresden and Chemnitz. In the long term, the cluster aims to become one of the world's leading locations for energy efficiency in electronics.
- *Logistics.* In addition to developing North Rhine-Westphalia's leading global position in the field of logistics, the EffizienzCluster aims to establish itself as a center for the innovative design of high-quality logistics services. There are approximately 120 companies and 11 research institutes working in the cluster. These include the Fraunhofer Institute for Material Flow and Logistics, the Technical University of Dortmund, and large and medium-sized enterprises.
- *Electric car engineering.* In the Electric Mobility South-West cluster, partners from the fields of automotive engineering, energy and supply

engineering, information and communications technologies and services, as well as the cross-section field production engineering are working on new concepts for electric mobility. The cluster's main projects include the design of battery production systems. Located in the Karlsruhe-Mannheim-Stuttgart-Ulm region, the cluster links 80 key players from industry, universities and research institutes, international companies, and SMEs.

SME Innovation Support Programs

Germany's High Tech Strategy also emphasizes the importance of creating more innovation opportunities for SMEs. Germany has established several programs recently to encourage SME innovation. These programs include the Central Innovation Program for SMEs, which connects SMEs directly with technical advisors; the HighTech Grunderfonds program, which provides venture capital; and the Signo program, which provides assistance in filing for patent rights.

- *Technical advisory services.* The Central Innovation Program for SMEs is the German government's largest program that supports innovation in SMEs by reducing the technological and economic risks of R&D projects. The program includes 100 technical advisors that help SMEs with eligible projects submit grant applications. Eligible projects are proposals for new products or processes that show high potential for commercialization, and contain technical risk. SMEs are matched with public or private nonprofit research institutions to conduct necessary research and development to explore possible ways to develop the new product. Initiated in 2009 and currently planned to continue through 2014, the program has an annual budget of $643 million and gives out about 4,000-5,000 project grants every year. Each grant covers 50 percent of the project costs, with the SME supplying the remaining 50 percent. At the close of each grant period, SMEs submit a report that details successes, challenges, and lessons learned in the process of attempting to develop the new product.
- *Venture capital funding.* The HighTech Grunderfonds program is a public-private venture capital fund that uses its annual budget of $411 million to provide support in amounts up to $643,000 to innovative start-up companies.
- *Assistance with filing for patent rights.* Signo provides federal assistance to SMEs in securing intellectual property for innovative products. The program provides support to SMEs in completing national and international patent applications. In 2012, the Signo program had a budget of $22 million.

Trade

Association of Chambers of Commerce and Industry

Germany's Association of Chambers of Commerce and Industry manages the country's largest export promotion effort. The national association brings together a network of 80 local chambers of commerce, which represent the interest of all commercial enterprises, with a focus on small businesses.[3] The Association of Chambers of Commerce and Industry and its funding agency, the Ministry of Economics and Technology, foster export activities in two main ways:

- *Selectively establishing partnerships abroad.* To establish partnership offices in foreign countries, the Association of Chambers of Commerce and Industry works through Chambers of Commerce abroad and meets with relevant stakeholders to determine whether German companies have sufficient interest in establishing an office. Currently, there are German chambers of commerce in 85 countries around the world. Annually, the Association of Chambers of Commerce and Industry has a budget of $219 million to manage the network of local chambers of commerce in Germany, as well as the partnership offices worldwide.
- *Providing assistance for trade fair attendance and participation in trade delegations.* According to German officials, The Ministry of Economics and Technology provides funding for businesses to participate in trade fairs around the world. The program supports SMEs in particular, but larger companies are not excluded from the program. Annually, assistance is provided for participation in over 200 trade events. The trade fair program has an annual budget of $54 million.

Training

Dual Training System

Germany's apprenticeship system—also referred to as the dual training system—provides post-secondary vocational education and training for students who wish to learn a skilled trade, and has several major features:

- *Combined on-the-job training and classroom instruction, according to nationally defined standards.* The program requires a combination of

---

[3] According to German officials, all businesses in Germany are required to belong to their local chamber of commerce.

on-the-job-training and classroom instruction leading to certification in any of Germany's 350 nationally recognized occupations. At the national level, industry associations and government officials negotiate the standards for certification as skilled in each occupation. At the state level, classroom instruction is formulated for each occupation.[4] Through the Federal Institute for Vocational Education and Training, the national government coordinates with industry groups to obtain input on the types of skills and training necessary, and then structures apprenticeships to meet those needs. According to German officials, this coordination was established by the Vocational Education Reform Act of 1969 (as amended in 2005). The executive board of the Federal Institute for Vocational Education and Training includes representatives from German unions, employers' associations, federal agencies, and state governments.

- *Nationally recognized credential.* As a result of the coordination at the national and state levels, the credentials obtained through the apprenticeship program are recognized by businesses and jurisdictions across the country.
- *Public-private cost sharing.* Employers pay apprentices a contractually agreed-upon stipend, with national unions and employer associations agreeing on the base apprentice wage in each occupation. According to officials from the Federal Institute for Vocational Education and Training. German businesses spent about $31 billion on apprenticeship programs in 2010.

Japan

Innovation

Next Generation Vehicle Program

According to Ministry of Economy, Trade, and Industry officials, the initial impetus for the Next Generation Vehicle (NGV) Program—a component of its Green Growth strategy—was to reduce carbon dioxide emissions and high energy prices.[5] More recently, the 2011 Fukushima disaster has

---

[4] According to German officials, in Germany, education policy is the responsibility of the states.

[5] The Ministry of Economy, Trade, and Industry and the Agency for Natural Resources and Energy are the main government agencies that administer this program. NGVs include hybrid vehicles, electric vehicles, plug-in hybrid vehicles, fuel-cell vehicles, clean diesel vehicles, and compressed natural gas vehicles.

focused attention on the need to reduce reliance on nuclear energy
without increasing imports of petroleum or natural gas.

Under the NGV program, private firms will manufacture the vehicles, but
the Japanese national government plays the following roles:

- *Setting targets for alternative-fuel vehicle diffusion.* The program sets
  a target for NGVs to comprise between 20 and 50 percent of
  passenger car sales by 2020, and between 50 and 70 percent by
  2030. The program also sets a target of 2 million normal chargers and
  5,000 quick chargers by 2020.[6]
- *Providing subsidies to encourage purchase of NGVs.* The national
  government covered half of the price gap between the cost of an
  electric vehicle and that of a gasoline model, up to approximately USD
  $12,500 since 2009 for electric vehicles, plug-in hybrid vehicles, and
  clean diesel vehicles. It also provided a temporary tax reduction of
  between 50 and 75 percent on acquisition tax and tonnage tax. The
  national government also subsidizes half the price of installation for
  the charging stations.
- *Establishing international standards for battery performance and
  charging systems.*[7] Japan's government is actively seeking to
  influence the setting of international technological standards, among
  competing models, for various components of the NGV, including
  battery performance and chargers.

Japan's national government works with regional and local governments,
universities, and/ or the private sectors in the following areas:

- *Conducting R&D for battery technology.* The national government
  collaborates with universities on related basic R&D, such as a

---

[6] A normal charger is built into each electric vehicle and requires eight hours overnight to
recharge a battery at home. Quick chargers can charge electric vehicles up to 80 percent
charge in 30 minutes. These chargers are for public use and serve as a safety net, for
example, if a driver is running low on battery power or if the driver is traveling a long way.

[7] International standards are generally developed through a process that is open to
participation by representatives of interested countries, transparent, consensus-based,
and subject to due process, according to NIST. NIST defines a standard as a document
that contains technical specifications or other precise criteria to be used consistently as a
rule, guideline, or definition of characteristics, to ensure that materials, products,
processes, personnel or services are competent and/or fit for their intended purpose(s).
According to the Japanese Industrial Standards Committee, standards specify size,
material, quality, and performance of products, among other things.

mechanism to analyze chemical response of batteries. However, for development of technology that will be commercially available in the near future, such as research on battery performance, the national government shares up to two-thirds of the cost with the private sector.

- *Supporting related infrastructure.* As part of its Green Growth Strategy, the private sector and local governments play a role in installation and operation of quick chargers. For example, car dealers offer memberships for quick chargers, and some local municipalities install quick chargers in their buildings and allow free use. According to Japanese national government officials, their role may include (1) developing the infrastructure for these chargers by contracting a private sector operator to form a network of charging stations; (2) developing a mechanism to charge users; (3) creating continuity in charger fees; and (4) ensuring payback to those providing these charger stations to accommodate the mix of actors and business models –some charging stations are free, others involve fees—and to ensure that charging stations are located in critical areas, such as along popular routes to rural/ resort areas.

According to Japanese national government officials, they plan to dedicate about 80 percent of the fiscal year 2012 budget to the subsidies that cover half of the price gap between the cost of an electric vehicle and that of a gasoline model and for charger installation. The remainder will fund the development of advanced batteries.

New Energy and Industrial Technology Development Organization

The New Energy and Industrial Technology Development Organization (NEDO) is Japan's largest public agency that promotes R&D.[8] It aims to promote the development and introduction of new technologies. Its programs and projects include: (1) promotion of research and development of energy, environmental and industrial technologies; (2) development, demonstration and introduction of promising technologies that private sector enterprises cannot transfer to the practical application stage by themselves due to the high risk and long development period

---

[8] According to NEDO officials, NEDO was reorganized in 2003 as an "incorporated administrative agency" under the Ministry of Economy, Trade and Industry, which sets its overall objectives. NEDO officials said that NEDO independently draws up plans to achieve the objectives and carry out its activities. NEDO is required to achieve meaningful program results and have them evaluated by external experts. Results are then reflected in management plans for subsequent years. NEDO is also required to publish its objectives, operation plans, and evaluation results and make them available to the general public, according to NEDO officials.

required; and (3) project management to assist in carrying out private sector projects.[9]

NEDO typically follows R&D priorities set by Japan's national government, but it also works with industry and universities to identify current trends and needs. It selects participants for its projects through a public solicitation process. Typically, NEDO connects university researchers and industry to collaborate on joint research. It may divide a project into different parts and assign responsibility for each part to a consortium of companies and/or universities. Research is conducted by the companies or universities, and project participants retain intellectual property, such as patents, resulting from their research.[10] After a project is complete and technologies are developed, project participants are mainly responsible for commercialization.

NEDO facilitates commercialization by coordinating research undertaken by the government and researchers and connecting relevant entities with potential users, according to officials.[11] NEDO, among others, is working to create a stronger link between R&D spending and profits. According to NEDO officials, its economic analysis illustrates a positive return on investment. For example, according to NEDO officials, annual product sales resulting from 50 outstanding projects have resulted in a return of seven times the initial investment. However, according to NEDO officials, they face challenges measuring concrete returns to taxpayers and in isolating NEDO's contribution. Therefore, they cannot claim that these returns are the direct result of their efforts.

---

[9] According to NEDO documents, NEDO is also responsible for acquisition of emission reduction credits through the Kyoto Protocol, which involves coordinating and promoting various projects to fulfill Japan's Kyoto Protocol obligation (6 percent greenhouse gas reduction compared to FY1990), among other things. According to NEDO officials, the Japanese government has not set an annual target or specific date to fulfill its greenhouse gas emission reduction under the first commitment period of the Kyoto Protocol.

[10] NEDO is public management agency; it does not have any research facilities of its own.

[11] According to Japanese government documents, efforts to integrate R&D across ministries and agencies with extensive collaboration between industry, academia and the government are part of Japan's national comprehensive strategy. NEDO has overseas offices in Beijing, Bangkok, New Delhi, Paris, Washington, D.C., and Silicon Valley. NEDO officials told us that these offices exist largely to conduct research on trends in other countries and to create partnership opportunities with foreign research institutes as well as to maintain and advance Japan's position as a global leader.

In fiscal year 2012, approximately 90 percent of NEDO's funding was used to develop technology for national R&D projects, including new manufacturing technology, new energy, nanotechnology, and materials, among others, according to NEDO officials. Less than 3 percent was used to fund commercialization and practical application activities, including technology innovation for small businesses. Other funding went to financial support for young researchers and activities related to the Kyoto Protocol Mechanisms. According to NEDO officials, NEDO typically provides funding of up to $12.5 million for 5-year projects.

Technology Advanced Metropolitan Area Association

The Technology Advanced Metropolitan Area (TAMA) Association is a regional cluster that supports local manufacturers by matching them with national, regional, and local interests to improve R&D and commercialization of technology and products. It is one of 18 clusters in METI's Industrial Cluster Project, which aims to strengthen over 10,000 regional SMEs and promote industrial clusters throughout Japan. The TAMA Association is a membership organization with approximately 300 manufacturing companies that focus on advanced technological and design capabilities or process technologies. In addition, it includes approximately 300 organizations and individuals that support innovations, including universities, financial institutions, local governments, and industry groups.[12] The TAMA Association provides its members with assistance services in the following areas, among others:

- *Creation of networks between large and SME manufacturers.* The TAMA Association produces a technical report that includes summaries of technology for each member company to help connect SMEs to larger manufacturers seeking the technology in which it specializes. After viewing the report, the large manufacturers contact the SMEs to improve existing R&D or produce product samples. According to one TAMA Association official, 170 SMEs have been hired for projects by large companies as a result of these activities in 2011.
- *Promotion of cooperation in R&D between manufacturers and universities.* The association supports R&D to promote cooperation between manufacturers and universities. For example, a manufacturer in need of a particular type of R&D would hire the TAMA Association to connect the company to university researchers conducting R&D in

---

[12] According to TAMA Association officials, it is Japan's first cluster that includes financial institutions.

that field. The TAMA Association also develops a network between SMEs, financial institutions, and research institutions to help a company develop a product or technology.

- *Support for creation of new businesses and technologies.* The TAMA Association relies on a network of about 150 experts, including consulting engineers and SME specialists, who support the creation of new businesses and development of new technologies by manufacturing companies. The TAMA Association helps SMEs apply for national government grants, and it works with financial institutions to provide funding for SME projects, according to a TAMA Association official. In addition, the association provides support to manufacturers that aim to enter a new field of business or commercialize technologies, including assistance with formulating business plans and acquiring business partners.

- *Development of marketing channels and overseas operations.* The TAMA Association works with experts to cultivate new markets for the region's technologies—in part through its overseas branches in South Korea, China, and Taiwan and its affiliates in Germany, Italy, Singapore, and the United States—to develop a network and products that assist manufacturers with formulating marketing strategies. In addition, TAMA works with SMEs to acquire patents for their technologies and advise companies on how to protect their intellectual property rights. According to a TAMA Association official, the organization has successfully assisted with 500 cases to commercialize products within the past 15 years.

- *Securing and fostering human resources.* Among other professional development projects, the TAMA Association accepts personnel to help other organizations learn how to better support local businesses. For example, local government or private sector officials may work for the TAMA Association for a 2-year period.

Kohsetsushi Centers/ Tokyo Metropolitan Industrial Technology Research Institute

Japan's Public Industrial Technology Research Institutes, or Kohsetsushi Centers, provide Japanese SME manufacturers with a range of services including technology guidance; technical assistance and training; networking; testing, analysis, and instrumentation; and access to open laboratories and test beds. They typically offer technical consultation services free of charge. Kohsetsushi Centers support Japanese SME manufacturers in adopting emerging technologies, including nanotechnology and robotics, among others. According to one Kohsetsushi official, all centers are geared toward supporting local industry; they do not specialize in particular industries. The Kohsetsushi Centers are generally funded and managed by local prefectures but are operated under the guidance of the Ministry of Economy, Trade, and

Industry. There are more than 180 centers throughout Japan—at least one in each of Japan's 47 prefectures—and more than 6,000 staff.

The Tokyo Metropolitan Industrial Technology Research Institute (TIRI) is one of the three largest Kohsetsushi centers in Japan. With a staff of about 275, it serves about a quarter of Tokyo's 40,000 manufacturers across three locations, primarily by providing services and information to SMEs, according to one TIRI official. TIRI serves not only SME manufacturers but SMEs in other industries, as well. In addition, larger enterprises may use TIRI's services, but they pay more for some services than SMEs. It is funded primarily by the Tokyo prefectural government, but 5 percent of its funding comes from the national government and another 8 percent from user fees.

TIRI's main support services include the following:

- *Technical assistance.* TIRI offers technical assistance including consultations and testing services and certifies test results. TIRI consultants provide advice and answer inquiries about technical problems free of charge by telephone or in person. In addition, TIRI tests products and parts to ensure they conform to industrial standards and provides non-standard testing upon request. TIRI conducts approximately 100,000 tests each year and has over 40 pieces of testing equipment for tests including temperature, acoustics, electromagnetism, humidity, voltage, vibration, impact, corrosion, and noise tolerance. For example, one TIRI official told us that a vacuum cleaner manufacturer might use the acoustic testing room to measure the decibel level of its products, and electronics manufacturers might test the ability of their products to withstand an electromagnetic shock (see Figure 4). According to one TIRI official, TIRI typically charges a nominal fee for testing services, but not for consultation. It also performs customized measuring and analysis services according to customer needs.

Figure 6: TIRI voltage testing room

Source: GAO photo.

- *Product development*. TIRI supports product development through rental laboratory space available 24 hours a day, experimental facilities and environmental testing equipment for shared use, and customer development support. TIRI also supports commercialization by supporting planning and design—such as branding for SME products—and prototyping of products using 3D printing technology.
- *R&D*. TIRI supports R&D, including basic, joint, and commissioned research. TIRI plans and implements basic research independently to develop new technology or to solve various challenges that SMEs face. The center also conducts joint research with SMEs for product and technology development. For example, small manufacturers often send one or two of their staff members to work on Kohsetsushi Center projects. This provides opportunities for company research personnel to gain research experience, develop new technical skills, and transfer technology back to their firms. TIRI also conducts commissioned research for which it receives external grants from the national government and other organizations. According to a TIRI official, the

center primarily follows the R&D priorities and policies set by the prefecture and TIRI, but universities and companies also contribute to that agenda. About 24 percent of TIRI's research is basic, 62 percent is commissioned, and 14 percent is joint.

- *Technical training.* TIRI has classrooms for seminars on product design and courses, for which students pay a fee, on new technology, industry trends, and internationalization. For example, officials showed us door knobs for home use that they helped one SME design. It offered this particular client assistance on usability, suggesting that they tilt the knob head to make opening the door easier. It also develops curricula and holds seminars to respond to needs from individual businesses or particular industry groups.
- *Collaboration between industry and academic researchers.* TIRI offers various services for connecting industry, academia, and public institutes. For example, it has instituted the Tokyo Innovation Hub to facilitate networking among SMEs and to promote cooperation between SMEs, universities, and research institutions. It also supports activities to encourage collaboration among more than 20 associations through its Cross-industrial Association.
- *Technology management.* TIRI offers support for technology management, including seminars and on-site technical support to assist with strategic development and technology management techniques. It supports the development of new products that utilize TIRI patents.[13] It also provides information to SMEs related to international standards compliance for clients who export products or enter into foreign markets.

TIRI tracks 12 organizational targets to measure its performance, including the number of patents acquired by TIRI and its partners, the number of products commercialized, and the number of licenses granted. Furthermore, it conducts a satisfaction survey of users each year. According to TIRI officials, these surveys illustrate that the center has successfully provided customer service but they face challenges with R&D output. However, they said that, generally speaking, their testing services have been highly appreciated by customers.

---

[13] TIRI can acquire intellectual property rights along with SMEs through joint research, and licensing TIRI's patents is a source of revenue for the organization.

South Korea

Innovation

Daedeok Innopolis and Daejeon Technopark

Along with two other centers in South Korea, the Daedeok Innopolis (Daedeok) is an innovation cluster that consists of universities, research institutes, government and government-invested institutions, corporate research institutes, and venture corporations. It receives funding from the national government—the Ministry of Trade, Industry, and Energy —but also generates revenue from private sector users. Focused on commercializing technology, Daedeok is the only science park in South Korea, according to officials.[14] It has five separate zones, each with its own specialized field, including a research complex, and other research institutes; an area for hi-tech firms; and an area for traditional manufacturing industries.[15] Various entities located within Daedeok have developed technologies that have been popular in the marketplace, including 4th generation (4G) mobile technology, and according to officials, the lithium ion battery, and a nuclear research reactor that put South Korea at the forefront of these technologies.

The Daejeon Technopark (Daejeon) focuses on the business aspects of a research institute, including growing existing SMEs and supporting R&D in the information technology, nanotechnology, robotics, and mechatronics industries. It was established in coordination with Daejeon city and the national government as an outgrowth of the Daedeok Innopolis, and it came into existence when it was designated as a special R&D zone.[16] While Daedeok focuses on technologies with great commercial potential, the Technopark focuses on smaller scale companies and more routine assistance, such as marketing, according to Daedeok officials.

---

[14] The other two centers in the foundation, Gwangju Innopolis and Daegu Innopolis, primarily focus on the optics and the information technology industries, respectively.

[15] Daejeon City—where both entities are located—was selected as the site for an International Science Business Belt in 2011, a government-sponsored project to foster basic science and potentially generate a South Korean Nobel Laureate. The project will involve a science research institute with 50 research groups and 3,000 employees.

[16] Daejeon is one of 18 technoparks across the country. There is at least one technopark in each of South Korea's 16 provinces, each taking on characteristics of the region.

Daedeok and Daejeon both provide support in the following areas for businesses that use their services:

- *Commercialization*. Daedeok networks with other regions and support organizations to promote its research results. Daejeon functions as a network hub between industry, academia, research institutes, and local government. For example, they connect SMEs to researchers or universities working on related research and provide SMEs access to technology.
- *Intellectual property rights protection*. Daejeon has a center dedicated to intellectual property through which they conduct research on existing technologies and trend analysis, support domestic and international applications, train companies on intellectual property protection, and support intellectual property planning for Daejeon City, among other things. Daedeok manages unused patents and evaluates new technology to match technology suppliers to potential customers.
- *Technology sharing*. For a fee, Daedeok provides facilities for various types of testing on product prototypes, such as electrical, temperature, or acoustic. Daejeon provides companies access to technology along with business expertise for consultation for SMEs. For example, during our visit, we observed testing of an electronic collection system (the technology used in "EZ Pass"-type cards) to see how it would perform under various speeds.
- *Training*. Daejeon provides a variety of training services for companies, both for new employees and continuing education on cutting-edge technology. Daedeok also provides training for start-up SMEs.

In addition to these services, Daedeok assists SMEs through grants and one-on-one consulting services, such as matching technology suppliers and customers, providing design services, and evaluating new technologies. Daedeok's R&D expenditures comprise 15 percent of the country's total R&D expenditures, according to officials. It houses 30 research institutes, 5 universities, and approximately 1,000 companies (mostly SMEs). The area is responsible for developing approximately 40,000 patents. For government-designed projects at Daejeon, the private sector typically shares 20 percent of the costs, according to Daejeon officials. Currently, there are about 2,000 high-tech firms, according to Daejeon officials.

One official noted that an assessment of Daejeon's equipment centers revealed that provide access to SMEs revealed that these centers are only being used at 40 percent of their capacity. The official said that the usage rate is not an area for concern because these centers are relatively new. The official also emphasized that the center responds to the expressed need from over 250 area companies. In addition, the official noted that with a new president taking office, Daejeon could face challenges if policy changes occur, but the official opined that policy changes are likely to be minor.[17]

Electronics and Telecommunications Research Institute

The Electronics and Telecommunications Research Institute (ETRI) is a global information technology research institute that works with the national South Korean government, the private sector, and universities to develop risky technology that the private sector is not willing to develop. It is the largest government-funded research institute in South Korea. ETRI, whose headquarters is located within the Daedeok Innopolis, collaborates with various institutes around Daedeok, such as research institutes focused on chemicals, energy, and satellites. It also conducts some joint projects with foreign universities, including some in the United States, and the private sector. These projects include research, technology transfer, research and business development, and training for foreign countries in areas such as information and communications technology.

ETRI is one of approximately 25 research institutes located within the Ministry of Science, ICT, and Future Planning. In calendar year 2012, the institute planned to spend almost 80 percent of its budget on government commissioned projects.[18] ETRI conducts more than 500 projects each year and employs approximately 2,000 people, the majority of whom are engineers.

ETRI is responsible for developing core information technology inventions, including 4th generation mobile technology, specialized handheld televisions, and a cancer diagnosis bio-chip for home use. The typical length for each project is between 3 and 5 years. ETRI measures success by the number of patent applications, amount of royalty income, number of international/domestic standards contributions, and the number of publications in science journals, according to one ETRI official. In 2012 and 2013, ETRI was ranked number one with the highest patent activity

---

[17] South Korea elected a new President who took office in February 2013, after our meeting with Daejeon officials.

[18] They also planned to fund government investments, royalties, and privately commissioned projects for companies such as Samsung and LG.

by an intellectual property trade journal, which cited approximately 540 patents in 2012 and approximately 700 patents in 2013.[19] The trade journal measures overall strength of patent portfolio holdings based on a combination of quality and quantity indicators, such as patents issued and science and research strength.[20]

Trade

Korea Trade-Investment Promotion Agency

The Korea Trade-Investment Promotion Agency (KOTRA) is the national implementing agency for Korea's trade and investment goals and policies set by the Ministry of Trade, Industry & Energy. It facilitates South Korea's economic development through various trade promotion activities, such as overseas market surveys and business matchmaking. It operates programs in:

- *Intellectual property rights protection.* KOTRA provides information about intellectual property right laws to firms that operate outside of South Korea.
- *Overseas marketing.* KOTRA develops and updates marketing strategies for South Korean products by the region and industry, and provides support to firms for their participation in exhibitions hosted overseas. KOTRA has also developed a "KOTRA global brand" program to support brand value to promote confidence in South Korean products that may be less familiar in overseas markets. KOTRA also hosts a global trade show to promote South Korea's major export products.
- *SME support.* KOTRA has more than 100 Korea Business Centers in approximately 80 countries that function as incubation centers. KOTRA also connects SME exporters to logistics companies—companies that help manage the flow of resources—in more than 20 major cities and regions worldwide to lower logistics costs for more than 2,000 South Korean SMEs.

---

[19] "IPIQ Innovation Anchor Scorecard (TM), Korea's Electronics & Telecommunications Research Institute Leads the Initial Ranking," *Intellectual Property Today*, 2012; and "IPIQ Innovation Anchor Scorecard (TM), Korea's Electronics & Telecommunications Research Institute #1 Again," *Intellectual Property Today*, 2013.

[20] Firms are measured against one another. Each firm's portfolio is measured on its technical strength, patents issued, science and research strength, and the speed at which technology become patent assets.

Appendix IV: GAO Contacts and Staff Acknowledgments

GAO Contact	Andrew Sherrill, (202) 512-7215 or sherrilla@gao.gov.
	Lawrance L. Evans, Jr., (202) 512-4802 or evansl@gao.gov.
Staff Acknowledgments	In addition to the contact named above, Laura Heald (Assistant Director), Kim Frankena (Assistant Director), Jaime Allentuck, Mark Glickman, and Cristina Ruggiero made key contributions to this report. In addition, key support was provided by James Bennett, David Chrisinger, Adam Cowles, Alexander Galuten, Jose A. Gomez, Ernie Jackson, John Lack, Kathy Leslie, Ashley McCall, Jean McSween, and Susan Offutt.

Related GAO Products

Export Promotion: Better Information Needed about Federal Resources. GAO-13-644. Washington, D.C.: July 17, 2013.

Export Promotion: Small Business Administration Needs to Improve Collaboration to Implement Its Expanded Role. GAO-13-217. Washington, D.C.: January 30, 2013.

Science, Technology, Engineering, and Mathematics Education: Strategic Planning Needed to Better Manage Overlapping Programs across Multiple Agencies. GAO-12-108. Washington, D.C.: January 20, 2012.

National Export Initiative: U.S. and Foreign Commercial Service Should Improve Performance and Resource Allocation Management. GAO-11-909. Washington, D.C.: September 29, 2011.

Small Business Innovation Research: SBA Should Work with Agencies to Improve the Data Available for Program Evaluation. GAO-11-698. Washington, D.C.: August 15, 2011.

Department of Commerce: Office of Manufacturing and Services Could Better Measure and Communicate Its Contributions to Trade Policy. GAO-11-583. Washington, D.C.: June 7, 2011.

Factors for Evaluating the Cost Share of Manufacturing Extension Partnership Program to Assist Small and Medium-Sized Manufacturers. GAO-11-437R. Washington, D.C.: April 4, 2011.

America COMPETES Act: It Is Too Early to Evaluate Program's Long-Term Effectiveness, but Agencies Could Improve Reporting of High-Risk, High-Reward Research Priorities. GAO-11-127R. Washington, D.C.: October 7, 2010.

America COMPETES Act: NIST Applied Some Safeguards in Obtaining Expert Services, but Additional Direction from Congress Is Needed. GAO-09-789. Washington, D.C.: August 7, 2009.

Export Promotion: Increases in Commercial Service Workforce Should Be Better Planned. GAO-10-874. Washington, D.C.: August 31, 2010.

Best Practices: DOD Can Achieve Better Outcomes by Standardizing the Way Manufacturing Risks Are Managed. GAO-10-439. Washington, D.C.: April 22, 2010.

International Trade: Observations on U.S. and Foreign Countries' Export Promotion Activities. GAO-10-310T. Washington, D.C.: December 9, 2009.

www.ingramcontent.com/pod-product-compliance
Lightning Source LLC
Chambersburg PA
CBHW080517290526
45790CB00006B/2207